Healthy Families

Healthy Families

A Guide for Parents of Children and Adolescents
with Sexual Behavior Problems

Timothy J. Kahn

The
SaferSociety
P R E S S

Brandon, Vermont

Printed in the United States of America
10 9 8 7 6 5 4 3 2 1

Library of Congress Cataloging-in-Publication Data
Kahn, Timothy J.
 Healthy families : a guide for parents of children and adolescents with sexual behavior problems / Timothy J. Kahn. -- 4th ed.
    p. cm.
 Includes bibliographical references.
 ISBN 978-1-884444-90-6
 1. Child sex offenders--Rehabilitation. 2. Teenage sex offenders--Rehabilitation. 3. Parent and child. 4. Families. I. Title.
 RJ506.S48K336 2011
 362.198'85836--dc23

                              2011037926

P.O. Box 340
Brandon, Vermont 05733
www.safersociety.org
(802) 247-3132

Safer Society Press is a program of the Safer Society Foundation, a 501(c)3 nonprofit dedicated to the prevention and treatment of sexual abuse. For more information, visit our Web site at www.safersociety.org

$12.95 plus shipping and handling
Order # WP148

Contents

Acknowledgments

I would like to thank my wife, DeeAnn, for her love and support over the past 30 years. She has been an inspiration and a positive role model who has worked daily to help our three children be responsible, caring members of society. I would also like to thank all of my staff and professional associates who have also worked very hard to help families recover from the discovery of their children's sexually abusive behavior problems. Krishan Hansen, Jo Langford, Carol Almero, Larraine Lynch, and Jenna Sandoval have all provided ideas, support, and guidance for this parents' guide. I would also like to thank Brent Oneal and Matt Platte for their ongoing collaboration and professional encouragement. I would also like to thank the staff of the Children's Response Center in Bellevue, Washington, the Harborview Center for Traumatic Stress in Seattle, and the King County Sexual Assault Resource Center in Renton, Washington, for their collaborations over the years in helping to reunify numerous families that have experienced sexual abuse between siblings. Special thanks go to David Walenta, Larraine Lynch, Jeannette Borunda, and Sylvan Bourgette for reviewing the *Healthy Families* manuscript and providing ideas and feedback that have proven very helpful. Finally, my heartfelt thanks to the many parents of children and adolescents with sexual behavior problems who have shared their pain, fears, confusion, anger, struggles, and hope during the past 30 years that I have worked in this field.

Introduction

If you are reading this book, you have likely discovered that your son or daughter has been involved in some problem sexual behavior that has affected another child, adolescent, or adult. You might even have learned that someone has brought your child to the attention of school or legal authorities. Coping with this experience will probably cause you considerable stress, fear, confusion, and isolation. Regardless, you can gain some comfort from the fact that children and adolescents who act out sexually are very different from adult sex offenders, and—with the right treatment—these kids often move beyond their difficulties and grow up to live happy, healthy lives.

We all know that sexuality is an important component of human existence. All humans have sexual feelings and behaviors. If your child has been involved in inappropriate or illegal sexual behavior, however, your child probably has stepped beyond the societal and ethical boundaries for healthy sexual behavior and may have done harm to another person or to several people as well as to himself or herself. This parents' guide will help you understand whether and why your child's behavior requires specialized counseling and what you can do to make sure that your child grows up to live a healthy and joyful life and does no further harm to others.

Current research shows that with proper assessment and counseling, most children and adolescents with sexual behavior problems can overcome their problems. Furthermore, most children and adolescents who develop sexual behavior problems do not grow up to be sexual offenders.

It is also very important to understand that current research about children and adolescents with sexual behavior problems clearly points to the importance of parental involvement if a child is to be successful in treatment. In fact, a great deal of research supports the belief that parents are far more important in the treatment process than is almost any other type of intervention, including specialized counseling, although those other modalities are also clearly important. Children and adolescents who have involved and committed parents—skilled in appropriate supervision and support—seem to do far better in treatment than children and adolescents who don't have that type of parental support. Simple strategies, such as providing close supervision or knowing your child's friends, can be instrumental in helping your child avoid further trouble. Unfortunately, such strategies are sometimes very hard to maintain, and they take a great deal of a parent's time and energy. This book's purpose is to provide the knowledge that will help parents implement and maintain such strategies.

During the first few weeks and months after becoming aware of a child's possible sexual behavior problems, parents often are overwhelmed by feelings of shame, fear, anger, disbelief, shock, and confusion. This response is normal and quite common. You probably can identify with part, if not all, of that kind of response. With patience, good guidance, support, and new information, however, you will learn how to cope with your feelings and how to rise to the challenge of helping your child or children overcome their sexual behavior issues. This book is designed to give parents a crash course on information and peer support as well as to provide practical steps to help their children reclaim healthy lives. Parents of children and adolescents with sexual behavior problems have to make many critical decisions about how to respond to their children's behaviors. This book is intended to give parents the knowledge they need to make positive, informed, and healthy decisions as they proceed through this process. *Healthy Families* is written for parents of children in outpatient treatment programs as well as for parents of children and adolescents who are placed in residential or institutional programs.

Over the past 30 years, many parents have told me that when they first read about this subject, they did not fully understand or use the information they were given. It was too much to take in all at once. These parents—who have been right where you are now—recommend that you read this book through once, then look at it again in a month or so, after some of the initial turmoil has settled down.

Experience, both with young children under age 12 as well as with adolescents, has shown that treatment is more effective when parents are active partners in the process. Reading this book and following its recommendations can help you be an active partner in your child's treatment. While reading this book is important, meeting with and developing a relationship with your child's counselor is probably even more important. Here's the reaction of one parent whose teenage child was court ordered into a treatment program:

> When my child first went to counseling, I didn't understand the importance of coming with him to treatment sessions. Going through the court process was very difficult, upsetting, and humiliating. After the court process, part of me just wanted to run away and hide. It was difficult to talk about anything at home. We didn't dare talk about what was going on.
>
> I found myself having difficulty concentrating at work, and I was afraid to go to church for fear someone would find out about what had happened in our family. I went to one counseling session with my son, but I was still resentful of the fact that I had to be in that office. I felt like I shouldn't have to be in counseling, because it was my son, not me, who had done the acting-out.
>
> I have since come to realize that I probably get more out of counseling than my son does. I now have someone to talk to, and I can share my feelings with someone who understands. I also realize that because I wasn't participating in counseling at first,

> I might have given my child the idea that I really didn't care, or that it wasn't really important. If I had my way now, I would recommend that the court make it mandatory for parents to get involved and to stay involved in the treatment process.

Also consider the reactions of a couple who adopted a seven-year-old boy who then started touching the private parts of other children at his school:

> We were not told that our adopted son had sexual-touching problems. It turns out that he had seen a lot of sexual behavior when he was very young. When he was expelled from his private school because of the sexual touching, both my husband and I were overwhelmed and scared. I was molested when I was a child, and my worst fear is that my son will grow up and become a sexual offender. I had a very hard time loving him after he started his sexual touching. Helping him to overcome his sexual behavior problems has been difficult and stressful, and overcoming my own personal reactions has also been very difficult. For a long time my husband had to take over parenting him, because I was too angry about what our son had done.

There is no question that parenting a child with sexual behavior problems is stressful, time-consuming, demanding, and sometimes emotionally overwhelming. This book offers step-by-step suggestions and guidance to help make this challenging process successful.

Since parenting a child or adolescent with sexual behavior problems is a complex, difficult job, you may have questions and concerns that are not addressed fully in this book. Whenever you have such questions or reactions, please write them down and share them with your child's evaluator or treatment provider at the earliest opportunity.

How to Use This Parents' Guide

This guide is designed to help assist parents in learning how to deal with a child's or adolescent's sexual misconduct. Parents should be provided with a copy of this guide as soon as possible after discovering that their child or children have acted out sexually. It can be given to parents of children and adolescents who are undergoing an assessment of their sexual behavior problems as well as parents whose children are undergoing specific inpatient or outpatient treatment for sexual behavior problems or sexual offending. This guide helps teach parents how to get involved and stay involved in their child's treatment program. It also helps parents understand many general principles of treatment and supervision for those children and adolescents.

This book is written for parents of children who are facing criminal charges for sexual misconduct as well as children who are not involved in the juvenile justice system. Foster parents and relatives, as well as staff at residential treatment centers, group homes, or institutions, may also find this book helpful. It is important to understand that children and adolescents with sexual behavior problems are not youthful versions of adult sex offenders. As we stressed earlier, compelling recent research demonstrates that the vast majority of young children with sexual behavior problems do not grow up to become adolescent sex offenders, nor do the vast majority of adolescents with sexual behavior problems grow up to become adult sex offenders. We can now be quite confident that with good counseling and education, parental education, and proper supervision, most sexual behavior problems can be successfully overcome, and our children and adolescents will move on to have healthy, successful lives. Have confidence that there truly is light at the end of the tunnel. This parents' guide will help lead you and your family down the path to a better life. Many, many parents of children and adolescents with sexual behavior problems have commented at the end of their treatment process

that there was a silver lining to their stressful and traumatic journey through the treatment and/or criminal justice process. They found that their children responded very well to treatment interventions, and they became more responsible, sensitive, and honest people in their day-to-day lives. Furthermore, parents have found that their family environments and family relationships became stronger and healthier, leading to an overall increase in family well-being.

This book is especially recommended for use with either the *Pathways* fourth-edition workbook, a guided treatment manual for children and adolescents between the ages of 10 and 19, or the *Roadmaps* second-edition workbook, a guided treatment manual for young people between the ages of 5 and 12 and older adolescents with learning problems or disabilities. Although boys with sexual behavior problems appear to outnumber girls by a large margin, researchers are identifying girls with sexual behavior problems more frequently than in the past. This guide and the *Pathways* and *Roadmaps* workbooks are all written to meet the needs of both males and females. Please note that it is not necessary for your child to be working in the *Pathways* workbook or the *Roadmaps* workbook for you to benefit from this parents' guide. The primary purpose of this book is to prepare you for understanding the investigation, assessment, and treatment process of your children or adolescents.

Getting to the Whole Truth . . . Eventually

As you read this book, you might be feeling confused, anxious, or even resentful that your child may be labeled a sexual offender or a child or adolescent with a sexual behavior problem. After all, your child may have been involved in something that seems relatively minor. While your reaction is understandable, the thing to remember is that you may be the least likely person your child will confide in regarding the full extent of his or her sexual behavior. Parents usually are the last to know the whole truth about their child's sexual misconduct. As your child goes through the assessment and treatment process, a more complete picture of his or her sexual behavior problems may emerge. It may turn out that your child's problems are greater than you thought, or that your child only has a minor problem that is easily corrected through education and good supervision.

You may feel in your heart that your child would tell you the truth because of the positive, open relationship you share. But generally, children and adolescents are very embarrassed about any sexual behavior—problematic or not. And when the behavior involves inappropriate actions, those children are afraid of being judged, rejected, and alienated from family members. Sometimes, they are even afraid of losing their home or being forced to leave home. They fear that their parents won't love them anymore if the parents learn of any inappropriate sexual behavior. Parents are often the last to learn about the extent of their child's sexual behavior, because it is easier for a child to tell a stranger (such as a counselor) about sexual experiences than it is to tell a parent.

First Steps Toward Help

The following suggestions are intended to help parents who have discovered that their child may have a sexual behavior problem:

- Reassure your child that you will love him or her no matter what sexual behavior he or she discloses. This step is very important for counteracting your child's feelings of shame, embarrassment, and fear, or his or her reluctance to talk about the issue.
- Be prepared for your child to deny any sexual misconduct. This response is normal. Full disclosure takes time, a great deal of support, and, sometimes, a certain amount of positive pressure and confrontation within a supportive treatment or evaluation environment.

- When your child does admit to having engaged in inappropriate sexual behavior, praise your child's willingness to talk about it. Tell your child that you will be there to help. Also tell your child that he or she should always be completely honest.

- Seek out details of the abusive or inappropriate behavior from the source. For example, if the parent of another child calls you to report misconduct, get the details. Write down the information to help you remember it later. Assure the other parent that you will seek appropriate help for your child.

- Sometimes a call back to the parent of the reported victim to offer support and to update the parent on actions being taken can do a lot to defuse anger and resentment. Many parents of victims never hear that appropriate steps were taken to get the abuser into treatment, so they assume that nothing was done.

- Emphasize to your child the importance of telling the whole truth, no matter what.

- Find professional help for your child and your family immediately. Do not wait for police or child protective services investigations. If your child has acted out sexually with another child in your family, seek immediate professional help for the victim as well.

- Develop your own personal support network. You likely will experience feelings of shame, anger, fear, and confusion as you go through this process. Talk to your close friends, relatives, and religious leaders. You may also need to see a professional counselor to deal with your emotional reactions to what is happening. Consider arranging a flexible work schedule at your job so that you can focus on family issues when you need to. Don't ignore your own reactions. Sometimes parents need to talk with a counselor of their own to handle this type of crisis in a constructive manner. It is important that you find a place to vent and process your emotions that is separate from your child. It may be too overwhelming to talk to other relatives about the situation. In this case it is important to seek out a parent support group for parents whose children are undergoing treatment. Even if their circumstances differ, they understand what you are going through and can offer support and ideas that help.

- Take care of yourself first, emotionally and physically. Make sure you get enough sleep and eat a healthy diet. Make some time for exercise. Go for a walk with your child or spouse. Avoid blaming each other, and reach out to others for support.

- Establish clear supervision rules within your home and take them very seriously. Do not let your child babysit for siblings or anyone else and never leave him or her alone with younger children. Provide constant visual supervision whenever your child is around younger children. The quality of your supervision at home may make the difference in decreasing opportunities for further abuse of a sibling, a neighbor child, or a schoolmate. Such supervision is even more important when your child is very young, between 5 and 11 years of age. Young children often have very limited ability to plan ahead or to anticipate the consequences of their actions. Very young children with sexual behavior problems often require complete auditory and visual supervision whenever other children are present.

- Many juvenile courts are implementing what they call 24/7 supervision, in which an adolescent who is charged with sexual misconduct is required to be under 24-hour, seven-days-per-week supervision by an adult who is responsible for and aware of the child's sexual behavior allegations. This high level of supervision is sometimes reduced after a thorough evaluation of the child's sexual behavior has been completed and if the evaluation shows the child to be at low risk of further sexual misconduct.

Most parents find that providing 24/7 supervision is a very difficult job. Here are some suggestions for appropriate family activities that one family came up with after their 15-year-old son was placed on 24/7 supervision for many months. Things to do while on 24/7 "line of sight" supervision with a large family of mixed ages that all will enjoy:

- Rearrange your house so you can see your child from more places. Same with your yard. Move your trampoline so you can see it from the living room.
- Go to the beach. (The beach is big and vast and all ages like the beach. You can see far so your child can be "alone" with friends or girlfriend.)
- Play at the local parks where there is lots of room to spread out while still in "line of sight").
- Go to G-rated movies (bored teens will go to any movie).
- Go bowling.
- Go outside and play sports like basketball or soccer.
- Go for a family picnic.
- Go for a family road trip to see local attractions.
- Go to the library and get lots of good books to read.
- Play a family board game.
- Learn a new card game.
- Play a family game with the Wii or X-box.

If your child can't leave and spend time at friends' houses because they are on 24/7 "line of sight," but friends can come to your house, here are some things to do as a "shadow" to your child that friends won't really notice as odd or controlling:

- Walk to the neighborhood park and play basketball. Say, "Oh you guys are walking to the park? We were just gonna walk down there, too." Then walk as far behind them as you can, both going and coming home.
- Walk to the neighborhood store. Say, "Oh we were thinking about walking down there too, funny!" then walk as far behind them as you can both ways.
- Rollerskating. You say, "I don't want to drive all the way home and then turn around and come back so I'll just sit here and read."
- PG-13 movies when allowed. "Hey, I wanted to see that, too. Don't worry, I will sit in the back of the theater."
- Go to large festivals, like powwows or local arts, crafts, or music gatherings. There is food and music.

Often parents are faced with difficult decisions while working with the authorities who are charged with investigating child sexual abuse reports, especially when the abuse has occurred at home. When the legal system is involved, it provides a necessary system of oversight and treatment support; in other cases, based on the particular circumstances, a legal case may be unnecessary for the health and recovery of both the victim and the abusing child. Occasionally, investigating officers may suggest that they are "trying to help families" when their job is really to investigate criminal conduct and refer cases to prosecutors, which may or may not be helpful in your particular situation. The main message here is to get good legal, assessment, supervision, and treatment advice from knowledgeable sources.

Not all parents of children and teenagers with sexual behavior problems want to become actively involved in their child's treatment. If you are experiencing resistance and personal negative reactions to the discovery of your child's behavior, please talk with your child's counselor to see if it might be helpful for you to find a personal counselor to help you work through your reactions. All parents of children and teenagers with sexual behavior problems should also find out from their child's evaluator or treatment provider if a parents' support or education group is available. If one of the parents was sexually abused as a child or adolescent, it is especially important for the parent to find his or her own professional therapist or counselor to help resolve the feelings that may emerge when that parent's own child discloses sexually abusive behavior. Even if you are not having a difficult time coping with this stressful situation, participating in a parents' support or education group is an excellent way to help you support and encourage your child's treatment. Such groups can be valuable for parents who are going through the crisis of discovering that their child has acted out sexually.

As the parent of a child or adolescent with a sexual behavior problem, you are no doubt experiencing a variety of feelings concerning your child, your family, the victim or victims, and the police or social services system. These feelings are often very intense. You may feel isolated, confused, alone, and angry because others don't understand what you are going through. In this parents' guide, you will read about the reactions of other parents who have had similar responses. You will also learn how you can play an important role in helping your child to resolve sexual problems and learn healthy and responsible ways to express emotions and sexual urges.

Consider the comments of this parent whose adolescent son had sexually abused her eight-year-old daughter:

When we finally started treatment, many of the most stressful steps were behind

us, but I still wanted to believe that we could get this whole thing over as soon as possible. I was wishing the process could go by quickly, but I also was overwhelmed as I looked at the work yet ahead for us. I struggled hard to accept that we might be in a better phase of this process, but that we still had a long way to go.

I hated having to share my responsibilities as a parent with a host of strangers in a very unfamiliar system—probation officers, attorneys, counselors. The process itself created enormous stress, fear, and paranoia. This response was in addition to the fact that our child had acted out sexually and had brought shame and embarrassment to our family.

I'm not sure when I finally accepted that what had happened was a life-changing event that would take a long time to absorb and that it would never be "done." It would have been better for me to realize that fact earlier. It is important to take the time to explore whatever resources are available, and to find the right professionals to help guide everyone through the experience.

I would tell anyone starting this hard process that you will be extremely vulnerable and will need help keeping your life together. It will be important for you to find someone to talk with outside the family, and you also need to try to have conversations within the family that do not focus on the nightmare at hand.

Be sure to take care of yourself: eat well, exercise, get plenty of sleep. It is absolutely necessary to accept help and to try not to be defensive as you learn to find your way through this difficult process.

Many treatment programs and counseling resources specialize in helping young boys and girls who have acted out sexually. Many use workbooks such as *Roadmaps* and *Pathways* to help educate and guide children and adolescents

through their treatment process. Such workbooks can be used with young people who molest (touch sexually) younger children, and they can also be used with young people who engage in forceful or harassing sexual behavior with others. Young people with poor boundaries who masturbate in public places, steal undergarments, are unable to avoid pornography, spy on others, make obscene phone calls, or run up huge phone bills calling sex talk lines will find such workbooks helpful and relevant. This guide will also help parents understand such sexual behavior problems and develop meaningful strategies for addressing them.

It is important that parents read and become familiar with any treatment handouts or workbooks that their therapist is using. If your child is in a residential treatment facility, it is important to learn about the rules and expectations in that facility. By reading such material carefully, parents will better understand their child's treatment. Treatment workbooks and manuals such as *Pathways* and *Roadmaps* are sometimes used in treatment groups under the guidance and supervision of trained and experienced treatment providers (counselors). Unfortunately, in some locations, such groups and counselors may not be available, and parents, their children's therapists, or the probation or parole officers will need to find other resources to help those parents cope with their children's sexual behavior problems.

Either way, parents play the most important role in their children's treatment since they generally know their children better than anybody else and they will be involved in those children's lives long after counseling is completed. A parent's support or lack of support for the treatment process will make a significant difference in his or her child's success.

It is essential that parents understand and support their child's treatment process. Children and adolescents with involved and supportive parents frequently require less time in therapy, learn more rapidly, and have lower reoffense or failure rates. That means talking regularly to your child's treatment provider, or getting to know the staff and therapists at your child's residential facility.

This parents' guide will provide many ideas and suggestions about how to build protective factors and resiliency into a family's life. This guide is designed to help parents make sense of the overwhelming legal system and understand how to address a child's sexual acting-out in a loving, caring, and positive manner, while appropriately attending to the needs of the other people who may have been hurt or affected by the child's behavior.

Chapter 1

First Reactions and Where to Turn for Help

In treatment programs and throughout this book, the children and adolescents who act out sexually are sometimes referred to as *clients*. A client can be any child or adolescent with any kind of sexual behavior problem. Terms such as *predator, perpetrator, offender, abuser,* and *adolescent sex offender* are generally not used in this book, even though many adolescents and some children with sexual behavior problems may face criminal charges in the juvenile justice system. Criminal charges may result in having those youth designated as sex offenders as a result of the formal court process. Some people argue that all children and adolescents with sexual behavior problems should be called sex offenders because, regardless of their legal status, they have offended against another person in a sexual manner, and the abuse they have inflicted on others can be traumatic. While there is no question that some sexual misconduct can be very damaging and negative, global terms such as those described above tend to support untested and invalid stereotypes about children and adolescents with sexual behavior problems. As we've stressed several times, most children and adolescents with sexual behavior problems *do not* grow up to become sexual offenders. Statistics show us that many children and adolescents with sexual behavior problems can and do grow up to live happy, successful, nonabusive lives.

One other comment about the use of the term *victim*: many victim advocacy groups find that using the term "my victim" tends to reinforce negative ideas about the offender possessing the victim, and it also tends to depersonalize the victim. Therefore, many treatment programs are encouraging children and adolescents to use

the phrase "the person I victimized" to help them be more respectful and compassionate. This may seem like a minor point, but it is important to help your child understand the reasoning behind the term. One of the key treatment challenges for victims is to help them overcome their view of themselves as victims, and help them view themselves in a more positive light, as a person who has survived sexual abuse. When clients refer to victims as "persons I victimized," they are supporting that effort.

As a counselor who has worked with children and adolescents with sexual behavior problems for the past 30 years, I would like to share some positive outcomes that inspire me to continue in this field. Many of my past clients have maintained periodic contact with me over the years, and I would like to share a few examples of their lives with you. Given the way the news media works, our clients will make first-page news whenever something horrific happens. They don't make the news when they simply learn from past mistakes and go on to live successful lives. Here is a brief list of what I have heard recently from some of my former clients who were in treatment for sexual behavior problems:

- One young man who repeatedly molested his younger sister when he was 14 years old has graduated from Harvard University with a major in English.
- One young woman who molested her younger brother when she was 12 years old is training to be a state trooper.
- Two young men with serious sexual behavior problems as young children

(under age 12) have completed military training and are serving in the marine corps in Iraq (they are in separate units; there is no connection between the two young men).

- One young man who molested a younger neighborhood boy when he was 13 has graduated from the University of Washington and is now attending medical school.
- One young man who molested several children he was babysitting around age 13 is happily married with two young children.
- One man who molested his younger sister at age 12 has married a woman with two children and is a very successful software engineer for a major software company in the Northwest.
- One young woman who molested three younger girls at age 13 and was convicted of a sexual offense (becoming a registered sex offender) became a cheerleader for her high school and went on to graduate from a community college.
- One young man who molested his sister at age 15 and became a registered sex offender went on to earn two master's degrees. He and his sister went through different therapy programs and resumed a healthy brother-sister relationship.

In the United States, as well as in some other countries, adolescents who act out sexually can be charged with serious crimes that are officially called sexual offenses. In Canada, children are only charged with such crimes if they are over the age of 12. In some states in the United States, children as young as eight can be charged with a sexual abuse crime, although in common practice children over age 12 are more likely to face actual criminal charges.

If youth are convicted of or plead guilty to a sexual offense, they will likely face many obstacles such as sex offender registration, in which they will be required to check in with the police at regular intervals and their names and information about their crimes will be included in county, state, or national registries. In addition, people in these offending youths' communities may be notified in person by law enforcement or by the mailing of flyers with his or her picture and information about the crime. In many places, a youth who is convicted of a sexual offense cannot attend any school that a victim or a victim's family member also attends, and the youth's own school will be informed of his or her sexual offense history. Since such requirements usually only affect sexual offenders, it is very important that we only refer to a youth as a sexual offender if the youth has gone to court and has pleaded guilty or been found guilty of a crime that is officially listed as a sexual offense.

Because of all the legal implications described above, many therapists also prefer to reserve the term *sex offender* for a person who has been formally charged with a sexual offense and has been found or has pleaded guilty to the offense in a court of law. Most children and adolescents with sexual behavior problems who have not been charged with a crime in juvenile or adult court retain all their rights to privacy, and the general public has no right to access information about their history. Children and adolescents with sexual behavior problems who have not been adjudicated for a sexual offense do not have to register as sex offenders. They also do not have to tell their school that they are a sexual offender, and they are not the subject of official notification to community members about their sexually abusive actions. Therefore, the term *client* is used to refer to both adjudicated (charged and convicted) sex offenders and nonadjudicated (not charged or convicted) children and adolescents with sexual behavior problems.

It may be very difficult for you to let someone else help your child with his or her sexual problems. One of the first steps in helping your child is to let go and allow the evaluator or therapist to take the primary role in your child's assessment or treatment. Once you have accomplished this kind of release, your support will be more effective.

Please take a moment to read a letter written especially for you by Jill, the mother of a 13-year-old boy who was accused of having sexual contact with his younger sister:

Dear Parent,

I am the mother of a child with sexual behavior problems, and I hope the following words will provide you with some comfort and hope. I remember the day we found out our son was accused of a sexual offense. We had no idea that his life was so out of control. We had thought of our family as fairly normal. We had challenges, of course, but we were coping—or so we thought. Neither my husband nor I had the skills to deal with all the upcoming issues: dealing with child protective services and the police, choosing a therapist, meeting a probation officer, or deciding what to tell our friends and family. We certainly could not tell anyone what our son had done. We worried about how family and friends would treat him and what they would think about us. So we tried to make all the decisions by ourselves, in between the tears and anger.

We finally made our way to this treatment program, two counselors and six months after the initial disclosure. What impressed me about the therapy was that there was a program, an organized approach to dealing with the issue of sexual abuse and related issues such as self-esteem, manipulation, honesty, and empathy. We as parents were involved; we were welcomed and included in the process.

My husband and I attended the parents' group beginning with our son's first meeting with his counselor. For us, it was not something we would normally do: bare our souls to complete strangers. To our relief, everyone there understood our feelings and nobody asked us to open up right away. Instead, they shared some of their own experiences, and we immediately felt that there was a light at the end of the tunnel. Those parents were coping, and many of them told us that things were actually improving in their families.

We had been told that it would help us and our children if we could bring ourselves to attend those meetings. In the end, we went, we cried, we listened, and we learned. We finally found a place where we could talk openly about all the complex issues involved in having a family where sexual abuse has occurred. We received acceptance, not judgment; empathy, not sympathy; knowledge, not theory. Eventually, we even experienced humor, something we thought we would never feel again.

Our son is now nearing the end of his treatment, and, in essence, so are we. I have attended the parents' group faithfully and now know so much more about parenting than I did before. I understand more about sexual abuse, and I feel that this will help our son in the future. I now understand thinking errors, minimizing, justifying, blaming—all are now routinely challenged. I would give anything for our family to have been spared this experience, but in the end, we have benefited, and our son and daughter have gotten the help they needed. Please don't wish for things to be the way they were. I don't anymore. I hope they are never the same again because, for me, the same as before means a child caught in a downward spiral, abusing innocent children, with us knowing nothing about it. Never again. Never again.

When we first found out about the abuse, we thought our family life was over—ruined beyond repair. But time heals, knowledge aids, and love rebuilds. I pray that for you there is a support group available that not only lets you vent all your emotions but also can help you learn, heal, and move on.

—Jill

Also consider the thoughts of one foster mother who has been parenting an eight-year-old child with sexual behavior problems for over two years:

> Don't let your guard down, even though what we have to do is very hard work. This has been a very isolating experience for my husband and me. I have learned that we are not the only parents dealing with this very personal problem. Don't give up or freak out just because you are dealing with your child's sexual behavior. Once you can get comfortable with the sexual element, it becomes just a behavior problem that warrants special attention. For the first year of dealing with our foster son's problem, we were in shock and we were constantly feeling overwhelmed by the intensity of the personal sexual behaviors that he was doing in our home and at school. We have since developed a wonderful support team of people who know of our son's problem, and we have developed a plan and hope for his and our future!

How to Find Help for Your Child and Family

The first step in helping your child is to find a qualified specialist experienced in working with children and adolescents with sexual behavior problems. If your child is charged with a sexual offense, he or she will need to be evaluated and treated by a specialist whose credentials and expertise are recognized by the juvenile or family court in your area. In some states, treatment providers must have a special license or certification. To find such a specialist, here are several suggestions:

- Call your local juvenile and family court and ask to speak to someone who supervises juvenile sex offenders on probation. Probation officers who supervise child and teenage sex offenders will know which therapists or programs the court and the probation department respect. This is an important consideration if your child is old enough to eventually be charged with a crime.

- Call a local sexual abuse agency that treats victims of abuse (look under "sexual abuse treatment" in the Yellow Pages or on the Internet). The staff there will usually be able to direct you to agencies that specialize in the treatment of people with sexual behavior problems.

- Call your local Children's Protective Services (CPS) or Department of Social Services (DSS or DSHS) office. Some CPS offices have access to family support partners who have gone through the system themselves and can help the family better understand the process. You can also take a look at *Rise Magazine* (www.risemagazine.org), which is a resource for parents who are involved in the child welfare system.

- Visit the Web site of the Association for the Treatment of Sexual Abusers (www.atsa.com). ATSA is the primary organization of professionals who evaluate, treat, or supervise adolescent and adult sexual abusers. The ATSA web site has links to other sites that may also be helpful; and it has a publications section and a public policy section where the public can have free access to current research reports and position papers that contain much helpful and current information about children and adolescents with sexual behavior problems.

- Visit the Safer Society Foundation Web site (www.safersociety.org). The Safer Society

Foundation is a nonprofit organization that (in addition to publishing this book and other treatment resources) maintains a treatment provider database and referral list for residential and outpatient treatment programs in North America. The foundation publishes many different treatment and educational workbooks and other materials that can be helpful to parents of children and adolescents with sexual behavior problems.

- Take a look at the Stop It Now Web site (www.stopitnow.com). Stop It Now is a nonprofit organization dedicated to the prevention of child abuse through public health approaches, including effective treatment. The Web site has many resources, including stories of hope from parents of abusers and victims as well as lists of questions and answers about sexual abuse.
- The NEARI Press is the New England Adolescent Research Institute, and their Web site is also useful (www.neari.com/press). NEARI publishes other helpful treatment resources and workbooks.
- Visit the Web site www.childmolestationprevention.org. This organization is based in Atlanta, and it maintains a list of therapists who perform specific evaluation and therapy for people with sexual behavior problems. The site also contains reading lists for parents of children with sexual behavior problems and parents of victims.
- The Web site of NCSBY, or the National Center on Sexual Behavior of Youth, contains helpful information about sexual development and youth with sexual behavior problems (www.ncsby.org).

If a child in your family has been the victim of an older child's sexual misconduct, it is important that you find a qualified counselor who is experienced in counseling sexual abuse victims and also has some experience with family reunification. Below are a number of resources that may be helpful in such situations.

Where to Go for Help

Several organizations can provide information and advice about child sexual abuse, including:

American Professional Society on the Abuse of Children
407 South Dearborn
Suite 1300
Chicago, IL 60605
(312) 554-0166
www.apsac.org

National Center for Missing and Exploited Children
Charles B. Wang International Children's Building
699 Prince Street
Alexandria, VA 22314-3175
24-hour hotline: 1-800-THE-LOST
www.missingkids.com

Child Help USA
15757 North 78th Street
Scottsdale, AZ 85260
(800) 4-A-CHILD
www.childhelpusa.org

Prevent Child Abuse America
332 S. Michigan Avenue
Suite 1600
Chicago, IL 60604-4357
(800) CHILDREN
www.preventchildabuse.org

National Sexual Violence Resource Center
1250 Maryland Avenue
Children's Bureau/ACYF
Washington, DC 20024
(800) 394-3366
www.nsvrc.org

Often a parent can find qualified sexual abuse counselors by doing a Google search on "sexual assault counseling centers," followed by the name of their town or city.

I Can't Believe This Is Happening!

When a child is accused of sexual misconduct or a sexual offense, it can be a nightmare for parents. It makes sense that you might feel overwhelmed, ashamed, surprised, upset, and frightened. You may have heard about other people who know young sexual offenders, but most likely you have not—in part because most parents don't talk publicly about their own children's sexual behavior issues. Because of the social disapproval or stigma associated with sexual behavior problems, these issues are not usually discussed openly. You most likely never thought it possible that you would be raising a child or adolescent with sexual behavior problems or one who has been defined as a sexual abuser or sexual offender. If you are like most other parents of such children and adolescents, you will probably look hard to find an explanation for your child's sexual behavior.

Sometimes, the first person abusers and their parents blame is the victim of the child's abusive behavior. Perhaps a victim has a prior history of inappropriate sexual conduct, or the victim's parents poorly supervise their child. Sometimes parents simply can't believe that their child could do something as awful as molest another child. In any event, it is important that you understand that victims are not responsible for being sexually abused. Your child is the only person who is responsible for his or her behavior. He or she may have learned the behavior from someone else, but in the end, your child needs to be accountable for the choices he or she makes. Just as the person injured or killed by a drunk driver is not to blame for the choices the driver made, neither is the victim of sexual abuse to blame for the choices made by a young abuser.

At the same time, specific circumstances may help to explain how your child gained access to the child victim or why your child chose to act out sexually. Certainly, most children and adolescents should not be held to the same standard of accountability as adults. Some children and adolescents with sexual behavior problems may be naïve sexually—that is, they just don't understand the implications of some of their own behaviors. They may also have general problems controlling impulsive behaviors that contribute to their sexual misbehavior. In addition, many children and adolescents with sexual behavior problems have learned about sexual behavior through being sexually abused, or by viewing pornography, either on television, videos, DVDs, or the Internet.

Many other factors contribute to the development of sexual behavior problems. The victim may have been especially vulnerable or might even have expressed interest in sexual matters. Your child may have developmental delays, alcohol or drug use problems, and other mental health problems such as depression, anxiety, bipolar disorder, or ADD/ADHD. Supervision in the victim's home and your own home might have been poor. Remember, however, that none of these circumstances alters the fact that your child made a choice to sexually act out—to evade supervision, to get access to a victim, to overcome the victim's resistance, and to complete the sexual contact and cover it up afterward.

Blame is not productive. Understanding, acceptance, and awareness are productive. By working to understand and change the factors that contributed to your child's sexual behavior and by building up your child's appropriate coping and decision-making skills, you will help decrease the likelihood that he or she will act out sexually again. There is every reason to believe that with good support, counseling, and supervision, your child's sexual behavior problems can be safely resolved.

Remember, you will probably be the very last person your child wants to talk to about his or her sexual behavior. Most children and teenagers with sexual behavior problems have a hard time being honest about their sexual behavior, even when talking with trained counselors. They have an even harder time being honest with parents (as well as friends and relatives) because they are afraid of your reaction, including possible rejection or anger. It is also extremely embarrassing and humiliating to admit to such behavior, especially in front of family members.

To help your child or teenager admit what has happened, try this approach: "I know you might not have told me everything about your sexual behavior. If you decide later to tell me more about what you did, I will still love you, no matter what you have done." It is very rare for children or teenagers to disclose the full extent of their sexual behavior to parents or even to trained counselors, at first. By telling your child that you will be there to provide love and support even if he or she has done other abusive behaviors or offenses, you increase the chances that your child will eventually tell you the whole truth. With the whole truth, treatment can be more effective in addressing all your child's issues, and if other victims are revealed in the process, they too can be encouraged to get help.

How Could This Happen?

As a parent, you may be wondering, "How could this happen to me and my family?" It is important to know that even the "best" families can have children and teenagers with sexual behavior problems. No doubt you are looking for a way to explain your child's behavior. You might think the victim lied or simply misinterpreted what happened, or even that the victim seduced your child. You may suspect or fear that your child has been sexually abused by another person. You may be thinking that your child's friends or sexually oriented Web sites and chat rooms taught or encouraged your child to engage in sexual behavior. This is where a skilled evaluator and therapist can help develop a better

understanding of all the factors that contributed in some way to your child's sexual behavior problems.

Keep in mind that sexual behavior can be very complex and that projecting blame is usually counterproductive. Your child made the final decision to act out, based on his or her life experiences and on the opportunity that was provided. Your child needs help to understand how and why he or she acted out sexually and also needs specific guidance in learning new skills that will help him or her make more productive choices in the future. As a parent, you may also need help and guidance yourself as you learn to cope with the revelation that your child may have engaged in sexual misconduct.

Consider the reflections of Betty, a teacher who learned that her son had molested her daughter as well as another child in her neighborhood:

> After a long five months of dealing with this situation, I still find it hard to talk about, even in writing. My wonderful son is a sexual offender! I know it helps me to pay attention to the feelings that have been troubling me, but I dread facing the pain again and the tremendous loss and sadness that overcome me each moment that I focus on this tragedy.

Betty found a trained counselor who specialized in working with families where sexual abuse had occurred. Betty found support, guidance, and help in coping with the stress and confusion she was feeling. As she, her son, and her daughter worked through the therapy process, Betty began to better understand how the experience had affected her:

> We did "all the right things." My son went to counseling. The family went to a family counselor, and I went to my own counselor. I also went to the parents' group. My son joined an anger-management group, and I read self-help books and worked on how

to feel comfortable and happy as a single person and a single parent. I continue to work on these issues today. My daughter was a victim, but she refuses to participate in any more counseling.

I received calls from the police at work. I sometimes had to leave work unexpectedly or with very short notice and rush home, as my daughter could not be left alone with my son, even for short times. If I had to go out and my daughter did not wish to go with me, I had to have an approved chaperone stay with them. Usually, I just made my son come with me, since sometimes there was just no other choice.

My employer and supervisors were understanding and helpful. They enabled me to meet these new family needs. They didn't seem to judge me or think less of me as a parent, as a person, or as a professional. Their support has allowed me to shore up my self-esteem, bit by bit. I am hopeful that with continued work, we can recover and learn to adapt in a healthy way to the trauma we have suffered.

This parents' guide provides specific suggestions and ideas for parents about how to cope emotionally with a child's sexual behavior problems. The guide also gives concrete guidance about how to better understand where your child's sexual behavior problem came from, and how to make sure that your child has adequate support in changing those problem sexual behaviors and developing a new healthy lifestyle.

Simple explanations for sexual behavior problems are often elusive. For example, one 12-year-old boy acted out sexually with a 5-year-old neighbor boy and was charged with a sexual offense in juvenile court. His evaluator found five factors that were involved in the development of his sexual behavior problems:

1. He was diagnosed with attention deficit hyperactivity disorder (ADHD).

2. He had been engaging in "cybersex" in chat rooms on the Internet.
3. He had seen a pornographic DVD at a friend's house.
4. When the sexual acting-out occurred, he was playing unsupervised in the neighborhood while his parents were at work.
5. Finally, he had started masturbating to ejaculation only a few months before the sexual incident, indicating that he was in the midst of pubertal changes.

Although the boy's evaluator found that all five factors played some role in the boy's sexual behavior problem, it was impossible for the evaluator to identify any one factor as the major motivator. Because sexual behavior problems are often multidimensional (as in this example), treatment and intervention programs also need to be multidimensional.

In another example, one seven-year-old boy was demonstrating inappropriate sexual touching of other students at school. He had been caught and disciplined several times, but the sexual acting-out was continuing. His evaluator found some key factors that were contributing to his sexual misconduct:

1. He had recently been adopted into a two-parent home, and, as a result, he had had to move from another state.
2. He had been in numerous foster homes before being adopted. In one of the foster homes, he had been placed with older girls who were sexually acting-out with each other, as well as with him.
3. He had had some significant symptoms of depression and was clearly unhappy and even traumatized about losing contact with his biological parents (whose parental rights had been terminated). In addition, he felt out of place both in his new home and in the new state.

Remember, a lot of help is available now for children and adolescents with sexual behavior problems. While parenting a child with such problems can be stressful and overwhelming, most of these children and adolescents can successfully overcome their problems and go on to live healthy lives. This parents' guide will help you work toward a positive outcome for your child and family.

Chapter 2

Understanding the Legal System

This chapter helps explain the complicated legal process that some parents find themselves in after their child has been involved in sexual misconduct. In the United States, some children under the age of 12 can be charged with crimes. In Canada, children under age 12 are not charged with any crimes. If your child is under the age of 12, and no legal charges are going to be filed, then most of this chapter will thankfully not apply to you. If your child has engaged in sexual misconduct and is over the age of 12, or is under 12 and is being investigated by law enforcement, then this chapter is especially important for you.

Many parents of children and adolescents with sexual behavior problems find the legal system to be confusing, complex, and frustrating. One parent commented that she found the legal system to be a "web of madness" that caused her considerable stress and difficulty after she discovered that her 13-year-old son had engaged in sexual behavior with her 6-year-old daughter. This chapter is designed to educate parents about what to expect when there is law enforcement or juvenile court involvement. Understanding how the legal system works is a good step toward helping your family cope with the discovery of a child's sexual behavior problem.

When your child is accused of engaging in sexual behavior that is against the law, and the victim or the victim's parents report the incident to the police or to the local child welfare agency, you can expect a law enforcement officer to eventually contact you and your child as part of the investigation. You may also be contacted by a social worker who works for your region's child protection department. If your child's sexual misconduct involved someone in your immedi-

ate family, you will likely be contacted by a child protection worker as well as a law enforcement officer. If your child is under the age of 12, law enforcement personnel may not be involved in an investigation, depending on the specific laws that are in effect in your region. Sexual behaviors that are against the law include the sexual touching of a younger child or someone who is cognitively impaired, sexual contact with someone who is under the influence of drugs or alcohol, any forceful sexual behavior or unwanted sexual touching, the theft of underwear or other personal items from someone's house or apartment, or the exposure of one's genitals to another person.

During a law enforcement investigation, your child may be taken to the police station for questioning or interviewed in your home or at school. During such an interview, your child will be asked to give a statement about what happened. Often, such statements play a large role in the prosecutor's decision about whether to file formal criminal charges.

It is usually advisable to seek legal advice from an attorney experienced in sexual abuse cases before allowing your child to be interviewed by a law enforcement officer.

In many jurisdictions, the victim and the victim's family don't make the decision to press criminal charges. The juvenile court prosecutor always makes the final decision about whether criminal charges will be filed, based on information provided by the police investigator. It is common for a victim's parents to tell the abuser's parents that they do not want to press charges, but formal charges can be filed anyway. This discrepancy is because the formal filing decision is always made by the prosecuting attorney, not the victim's parents.

Because sexual abuse charges can be emotionally loaded and difficult to understand, and they may have significant implications for the entire family, it is important for you, as a parent, to get competent legal advice to protect your parental rights and your family. Try to hire an attorney who is experienced in dealing with children and adolescents who are charged with sexual offenses. In most jurisdictions, special laws apply to sexual offenders; it is important that your attorney knows exactly what to expect as your child goes through the court system. If you do not have the financial resources to hire an attorney, call your local juvenile court and ask how to contact the public defender organizations in your area. A public defender may be able to give you advice about how to respond during the initial investigation.

Parents as well as children and adolescents can sometimes be very confused by the legal process. For example, it is common for attorneys to advise their clients to plead not guilty during the first court hearing. This plea gives the attorney time to talk with the prosecutor and try to negotiate for a lesser charge or a lighter punishment. Since this process can be confusing—especially when a child has already admitted to the sexual misconduct—parents, attorneys, and treatment providers need to have good and ongoing communication with the child to help him or her understand what is happening.

Parents often have to make a critical early decision about whether or not to seek professional help for their child's sexual behavior problem. Here is an example of one family's decision process: The parents of a 15-year-old boy were told by their 11-year-old daughter that their son had been touching her inappropriately. The parents turned to their church for advice, and were informed that if church personnel were told about what had happened, the church staff would have to report the situation to both the police and the social services department. The parents, concerned about having their son prosecuted for a sexual offense, chose instead to send their son to live with a grandparent. The family decided to handle the situation alone, without professional counselors.

The parents thought they had made the right decision until several years later when their other daughter disclosed to a school counselor that the son had also been doing sexual things to her. The school counselor made a report to the local social services department, and the son ended up being interviewed by the police. After a long investigation, the son, who was by then 20 years old, admitted to also having had sexual contact with a neighbor boy, in addition to extensive sexual contact with his younger sisters that the girls had previously not revealed to the parents. The young man was then charged with several sexual offenses in adult court. When he was finally sentenced, he was given six months in jail, and ten-years-to-life adult probation. He had become an adult registered sex offender, and most parts of his life were now controlled by his Department of Corrections probation officer.

In hindsight, the parents of this young man felt extremely guilty and regretful about the choices they had made. Had they gone to authorities and sought professional help when he was 15, he likely would have been charged as a juvenile offender and would have been offered counseling and only one to three years of probation. In this young man's case, he eventually admitted that he had engaged in some sexual misconduct even after he was sent to a grandparent's house. In this case, simply changing his living situation had not been enough to stop his problem sexual behavior.

The other even more important consideration in this example is that the parents did not offer their daughters an opportunity to disclose what had happened to them. As is very common with sexual abuse victims, the daughters felt extremely embarrassed and ashamed and did not want to cause further trouble by telling everything their brother had done to them. By the parents not seeking professional help for their children, the daughters lived with their shame, guilt, and embarrassment for several years before learning that their feelings were normal and that they were not to blame for what their brother had done with them.

The critical message here is to always immediately seek professional help both for the child who has acted out sexually AND for the victim or victims of the sexual misconduct.

How the Legal System Works

Every country in the world and all states in the United States have distinct legal systems. While many similarities exist between those various systems, some significant differences are also present.

In most places, legal systems include a prosecuting attorney who is employed by the government. It is that person's job to review police reports and make decisions about what, if any, legal charges to bring against a person who is accused of breaking the law. The investigating police officers collect witnesses' and victims' statements, and then they forward that information to the prosecuting attorney. The police officers may make a recommendation about formal criminal charges, but the prosecuting attorney will make the final decision about the charges.

It is important to understand that in some areas the investigation process can occur quickly, and a formal charging decision can be made within several weeks or months. It is not uncommon, however, for the investigation and charging process to take a year or longer. Many, many parents have mistakenly thought that no charges were going to be filed, only to find out months later that their child was being charged with a crime. Usually, parents find out about such decisions when they check their mail and find that the local juvenile court has sent them a summons to have their child appear in court. If the parents have retained an attorney, it is sometimes possible for the attorney to monitor the progress of the potential charges involved, and the parents

may then be able to negotiate with the prosecuting attorney before a formal charge is made. Experienced attorneys will usually recommend that parents seek a professional evaluation by licensed or experienced sexual abuse or sexual behavior counselors who are respected by juvenile court authorities. If the prosecuting attorney sees that the child's parents are seeking appropriate evaluation and treatment, the prosecuting attorney may be more inclined to offer a reduced charge.

One of the most important things for parents to know is that most prosecuting attorneys can select from a list of various laws as they make decisions about which legal offenses they feel are appropriate to bring against a child. The list of laws will most likely include crimes defined legally as sexual offenses, but the list may also include laws that are not legally defined by that terminology. If your child is charged with and then pleads guilty to or is convicted of a sexual offense, many new requirements and procedures will be placed on him or her and will immediately take effect. For example, most states in the United States have sex offender registration laws that require sexual offenders, even juvenile sex offenders, to register on law enforcement and Internet registries. In some cases, that information is available to the public.

Every state has somewhat different laws regarding this step in the process. For the most up-to-date information, perform a Google or other Internet search on "adolescent sex offense registration laws." You may also wish to consult the Prevent Abuse Now Web site (www.prevent-abuse-now.com/register.htm) for a state-by-state directory of adolescent sex offender registration laws and directories.

Washington State's 1990 Community Protection Act included America's first law authorizing public notification when dangerous sex offenders are released into the community. However, it was the brutal 1994 rape and murder of seven-year-old Megan Kanka that resulted in public demand for broad-based community notification. On May 17, 1996, President Clinton signed Megan's Law. Megan's Law requires the following two components:

Sex Offender Registration–The 1994 Jacob Wetterling Act requires states to register individuals convicted of sex crimes against children. The law states that sex offender registration laws are necessary because:

- Sex offenders pose a high risk of reoffending after release from custody (Author's note: According to current research, this repeat offending is not necessarily true of juvenile sex offenders, but it is still what the law states);
- Protecting the public from sex offenders is a primary governmental interest;
- The privacy interest of people convicted of sex offenses is less important than the government's interest in public safety; and
- Release of certain information about sex offenders to public agencies and the general public will assist in protecting the public.

Community Notification–Megan's Law allows states the discretion to establish criteria for disclosure, but it compels them to make private and personal information on registered sex offenders available to the public. Community notification is intended to:

- Assist law enforcement in investigations;
- Establish legal grounds for monitoring known offenders;
- Deter sex offenders from committing new offenses; and
- Offer citizens information they can use to protect children from victimization.

Parents can check the Klaas Kids Foundation (www.klaaskids.org/pg-legmeg.htm) for a frequently updated directory of community notification laws in each state. Remember, each state has somewhat different laws and requirements.

On July 27, 2006, President Bush signed the Adam Walsh Child Protection and Safety Act. One important component of that act requires the Justice Department to create a publicly accessible, Internet-based, national sex offender database that allows users to search for sex offenders across state lines. The result is the Dru Sjodin National Sex Offender Public Website (www.nsopr.gov).

The Adam Walsh Act may result in significant long-term changes for juvenile sex offenders in the United States. SORNA, which is the Sex Offender Registration and Notification Act, is also known as Title I of the Adam Walsh Child Protection and Safety Act of 2006 (Public Law 248-109). SORNA provides a comprehensive set of minimum standards for sex offender registration and notification in the United States. SORNA aims to close potential gaps and loopholes that existed under prior laws; it generally strengthens the nationwide network of sex offender registration and notification programs. Important areas of reform under SORNA include that the law:

- Extends the jurisdictions in which sex offender registration is required beyond the 50 states, the District of Columbia, and the principal U.S. territories to include federally recognized Indian tribes;
- Incorporates a more comprehensive group of sex offenders and sex offenses for which registration is required;
- Requires sex offenders to register and keep their registration current in the jurisdictions in which they reside, work, or go to school;
- Requires sex offenders to provide more extensive registration information;
- Requires sex offenders to go to local police agencies in person to verify and update their registration information;
- Expands the amount of information available to the public regarding registered sex offenders; and
- Makes changes in the required minimum duration of registration for sex offenders.

For example, SORNA requires that most adolescent sex offenders who offend against younger children and are over the age of 14 when they commit the offense must register for 25 years. After 25 years, the registration requirement may be discontinued if the client has successfully completed a treatment program. As of 2011, not all states had fully implemented SORNA changes, so it may be some time until all the changes are made. Some states may not implement parts of that law at all.

What Are Level 1, Level 2, and Level 3 Sexual Offenders?

Most states have adopted sex offender notification levels that are designed to distinguish between high-risk and low-risk sex offenders. The levels generally work as follows:

At Level 1, the designation of offender generally means that the person has a low risk of committing another sex crime. At Level 2, the designation of offender generally means that the person is at a moderate risk of committing another sex crime. And at Level 3, the designation of offender means that the person has a high risk of committing another sex crime.

It should be noted that while states are trying to find valid ways of assessing risk of further sexual offenses, this levels approach is very controversial when it comes to adolescent sex offenders. It is very difficult to find valid risk assessment tools, and some researchers question whether it is possible to accurately assess an adolescent sex offender's risk of future offenses, due to how rapidly adolescents change and how dependent they are on their living environment.

In some jurisdictions, public meetings are held whenever a Level 2 or Level 3 sex offender moves in to a community. Generally, Level 2 and Level 3 sex offenders are subject to the greatest publicity and public concern. Level 1 sex offenders are often placed on a registry, but detailed information about them is often not easily available to the general public. Information about Level 2 and Level 3 sex offenders is often available on the Internet.

What Is Sex Offender Registration?

Sex offender registration is when a convicted sexual offender must go to the local police agency and provide detailed information about his or her residence and place of employment or schools attended. Current pictures are taken of that offender. Some sex offenders, usually the Level 2 and Level 3 offenders, must return to the law enforcement office every 90 days to update their information. With Level 1 sex offenders, local law enforcement agencies may visit the offender's home once a year or may ask that the offender send in a form once a year to update personal information. These procedures vary widely from state to state in the United States, and other countries may or may not have any sex offender registry. With sex offender registration, information about a sex offender's crimes becomes public information, and the public is often provided with a picture of the offender, the person's specific address or at least a general area where that person is living, and other background information.

What Is Failure to Register?

Failure to register is when a sex offender who is required to register does not do so in a timely manner. Usually sex offenders are required to update their information any time they move to a different address or change schools. Failure to register is usually considered a new crime—often a felony—which is one of the most serious types of crimes. Many adolescent sex offenders do not adequately understand this requirement, and they get sloppy or lazy about following this rule. This can be very unfortunate, because failure to register often results in immediate incarceration, another period of probation, and a requirement to continue to register as a sex offender for another lengthy period.

Does the Sex Offender Registration Requirement Ever Go Away?

The Adam Walsh Act requires 25 years of sex offender registration for teenagers who are over 14 at the time of their offense against a younger child. It appears that there is no way to have that registration requirement dismissed prior to the 25-year cutoff point. In addition, the law also requires that the offender successfully complete a treatment program. The Adam Walsh Act is not fully implemented in each state, however, as of 2011. Some states may not require all juvenile sex offenders to register, and other states still have provisions that allow teenage sex offenders to petition the court for dismissal of registration, sometimes as soon as they have successfully completed a treatment program.

As of 2011, 20 states have some form of discretion to determine whether a juvenile should be subject to registration or exempted from registration. In some states, judges have the discretion to determine whether or not the juvenile will be required to register or will be exempted from registration.

In many states, sexual offenders are required to hire an attorney to accomplish dismissal of the sex offender registration requirement. Given this, it is important that teenager sex offenders be encouraged to save money for this effort, because it is sometimes difficult to find public defenders to file the necessary paperwork and to attend the court hearing to accomplish this task. Of course, the most important thing is to make sure that the teen first successfully completes a recognized sexual offender treatment program. Some states have certification or licensing requirements for sex offender treatment providers. It is very important that parents find a well-qualified treatment provider who is licensed or certified in their state.

What Is Probation and Parole?

Probation refers to a period of time that a youth is supervised by a probation counselor or probation officer who works for a juvenile court. Probation involves oversight by a judge, who can impose consequences if the probation conditions are not met. Usually, probation orders contain very strict and specific rules about what a client can or cannot do. Some probation orders include a curfew. Many probation orders require that

clients attend counseling, attend school, refrain from using drugs or alcohol, and stay away from younger children. It is important to understand that each of the probation rules carries the weight of the judge's order, and any violation of those probation rules will result in a new court hearing and possibly time in juvenile detention.

In some cases, clients receive suspended sentences that allow them to stay in the community, but they can be sent to a juvenile correctional institution if they do not follow probation conditions. Judges also can order clients to spend time in detention facilities for violations, or they may impose a wide variety of other sanctions, such as community service or lifestyle restrictions.

Parole refers to a period of time that follows incarceration in a juvenile institution. A parole officer typically works for the state or county Department of Juvenile Corrections. Violations of parole result in hearings with juvenile corrections staff and sometimes with an administrative judge. Parole violations can result in many different types of consequences, including that the length of time an offender is on parole might be extended or that the offender might even have to be returned to an institution. Supervision of clients when vulnerable people (such as younger children) are present is usually one of the most seriously enforced conditions of probation or parole.

Parents and their children and adolescents should always closely study the probation and parole rules, to make sure that every one of them is being followed.

What Happens in Juvenile Detention or a Juvenile Corrections Facility?

Many adolescents who are charged with a sexual offense will likely spend at least a few days in a juvenile detention facility. The majority of juvenile detention facilities in the United States are reasonably safe, and adolescents will experience the time there as somewhat boring. Remember that time in juvenile detention is designed to be punishment and a consequence for the child's poor choices. Parents are often very fearful about their child going to detention or a juvenile corrections facility, but the reality is that most facilities in most parts of the United States are very well supervised and reasonably safe. Clients usually report that their time in detention facilities was boring and uneventful, but perhaps helpful at reminding them of what is at stake in their situation.

What Are Conditions of Release?

Some courts issue conditions of release after a client first enters a plea to an offense. Instead of putting the teen in juvenile detention until the trial, the judge imposes conditions of release that will remain in effect until the youth's trial or sentencing hearing. These conditions of release are very much like the probation rules described above. Failure to follow any of the conditions of release will result in another court hearing and the strong possibility that the teen will be put into juvenile detention. Many juvenile courts are now imposing 24/7 supervision rules on adolescent sex offenders, meaning they must be supervised 24 hours a day, 7 days a week by a responsible adult who is aware of their charges.

What Is a Plea Bargain?

A plea bargain is when a defense attorney works with a prosecutor to get the prosecutor to amend or change the legal charges against a client. This process can happen at any time up until a judge makes a finding of guilt or innocence against a client. Prosecutors usually charge the most serious offense that the evidence supports, but they may be willing to reduce the charge in a number of situations, such as if the evidence is weak, if the victim's parents do not support the higher charge, if the prosecutor believes the offender is low risk, or if the prosecutor is impressed with how an offender's family is seeking help on its own.

In a plea bargain, the defense attorney is often trying to convince the prosecutor to reduce the charge to one that is not considered a sexual offense. For example, in Washington State, one of the most popular plea bargains is to reduce

a felony sex offense to a charge called Assault in the Fourth Degree with Sexual Motivation. This charge is not a felony. It is instead considered a gross misdemeanor (the second most serious type of offense). If a teenager ends up being charged with a gross misdemeanor, he or she would not have to register as a sexual offender in Washington State, no community notification would be required, and the charge could be sealed when the teenager turns 18. The lesser charge, however, still could result in the offender having almost the same probation and treatment requirements as a felony sex offense charge.

Many states have similar options that allow a prosecutor some discretion in how to charge a given case. A plea bargain is when defense attorneys work with prosecutors to find alternative charges that might provide a court sanction without affecting a teenager's future as dramatically as a felony sex offense charge.

What Is a Sexual Assault Protection Order?

A Sexual Assault Protection Order is a civil order issued by the court on behalf of a sexual assault victim. Laws governing Sexual Assault Protection Orders vary by state. The order can require the alleged perpetrator to stay away from the victim or places where the victim lives, goes to school, or works, and to have no further contact with the victim. In practice, a Sexual Assault Protection Order can require that a juvenile offender's family move to a different location. In a recent case in Washington State, a 17-year-old boy had molested a 6-year-old female child in the neighborhood of his family home. Several days before the boy was to be released from a juvenile institution, the victim's family was granted a Sexual Assault Protection Order that required the teenage offender to remain several thousand feet away from the victim's home, school, and daycare at all times. This meant that the boy could not live in his parents' home, and the parents had to live in a motel for several weeks until they could put their home up for sale and move to a new home.

A Sexual Assault Protection Order may also

be obtained as part of a criminal case. If a victim reports the sexual assault to law enforcement and the offender is being prosecuted, a judge may order a Sexual Assault Protection Order to keep the assailant away from the victim when the assailant is released from custody.

Sexual Assault Protection Orders are rapidly gaining favor in the United States. In 2006, Washington State became the 13th state to adopt a specific law establishing a Sexual Assault Protection Order. According to the American Bar Association, as of 2009 17 states had adopted laws establishing Sexual Assault Protection Orders. It is expected that many other states will follow in coming years. To find out about current laws in your state, do a Google, Bing, or Yahoo search on "Sexual Assault Protection Orders" followed by the name of your state. This search should give you current information about similar laws where you live.

What Is an Immunity or Derivative Use Immunity Order?

Immunity from prosecution occurs when a prosecutor or judge grants immunity, usually to a witness, in exchange for testimony or production of other evidence. It is immunity because the prosecutor essentially agrees to never prosecute the crime that the witness might have committed in exchange for the witness testifying truthfully about what happened.

The prosecutor or judge may grant immunity in one of two forms: *Transactional immunity* (colloquially known as "blanket" or "total" immunity) completely protects the witness from future prosecution for crimes related to his or her testimony. *Use and derivative use immunity* prevents the prosecutor or judge only from using the witness's own testimony or any evidence derived from the testimony against the witness. However, should the prosecutor acquire evidence substantiating the supposed crime—independently of the witness's testimony—the witness may then be prosecuted for the crime.

Here is how this sometimes works in juvenile sex offense cases. In some places, defense attorneys ask the prosecutor or judge for a Use and Derivative Use Immunity Order before their client goes through a sexual behavior evaluation and risk assessment. This is because it is very common for adolescents to disclose more incidents of abuse or more victims of abuse during an evaluation process. By having a Use and Derivative Use Immunity Order in place, the client cannot be prosecuted for behavior he or she discloses during the evaluation process, if the resulting investigation turns up evidence of the abuse. It should be noted that the Use and Derivative Use Immunity Order does not affect the mandatory reporting obligation of counselors or evaluators, and it does not affect the sexual abuse investigation process.

The Use and Derivative Use Immunity Order comes into play when charges are filed against the client who made the disclosure, and the Use and Derivative Use Immunity Order prevents those charges from going through the court process. When clients have a Use and Derivative Use Immunity Order in place, it is usually in their best interest to disclose all previous sexual acting-out, because if they disclose it, they likely will not face further criminal charges, but if they don't disclose the behavior and one of the victims reports the abuse first, then they can be charged with a new crime and the Use and Derivative Use Immunity Order will have no effect.

If your child is going through a sexual behavior evaluation process, it is often a good idea to ask the attorney if it is possible to obtain a Use or Derivative Use Immunity Order. In some parts of the country, such orders are common, but in other areas Use and Derivative Use Immunity Orders are less common.

What Is the Risk of a Civil Suit?

A *civil suit* is when a victim or the victim's family goes to court to gain financial judgments from the client or client's family. Civil suits are separate from criminal charges, and it is possible for an adolescent sex offender to go through the legal system with criminal charges, and then also be sued later by the victim's family. Civil suits often take years to work their way through the court system, and they are always a stressful experience for both adolescents and parents.

One of the best ways to avoid a civil suit is to always seek and follow professional advice after discovering that your child has acted out sexually. By seeking immediate professional advice you probably will avoid being accused of negligence, which is a common accusation in a civil suit. For example, if parents find out about their child's sexual behavior problem, but then they fail to provide needed supervision, those parents could be opening the door to a civil suit if their child acts out again in the future.

Chapter 3

Common Questions

Parents of children and adolescents with sexual behavior problems often ask the following questions:

How can I tell the difference between what is normal sexual behavior during childhood and what might be abusive or inappropriate?

It can take training and experience to determine whether a particular incident was innocently explorative, abusive, or victimizing. Children often experiment with sexuality by playing touching games with one another. Some guidelines may be helpful to you as a parent. If the answer to any of the following questions is yes, the sexual incident was probably not simple experimentation, and it will warrant further assessment by a specialist:

- Was one of the children in the encounter more than two years older than the other or bigger or more aggressive, regardless of the age difference? Abusive contact relies on the abuser having more power and knowledge than the victim. Sometimes that power comes from age and experience, but not always. Even children close in age can be involved in abusive sexual behavior if one has more power or knowledge and is willing to use it in an aggressive or coercive way.
- Did the sexual encounter involve intrusive sexual contact such as oral, vaginal, or anal penetration by a penis, finger, or other object (pen, candle, toy, bottle, stick)?
- Did one of the children use force, tricks, coercion, bribes, or threats to gain the compliance of the other?

- Has one of the children been involved in sexual behavior previously, and has he or she continued it despite being told to stop?

Curiosity about the look or feel of sexual organs is normal, particularly when the children are under age 7. It is normal for children to say and do things like, "I'll show you mine if you show me yours." Children who are simulating adult sexual behavior, however, have almost always been previously exposed to it by being sexually abused or by watching others engaged in sexual behavior, either in person or in television programs, movies, magazines, or on the Internet, or by listening to or participating in telephone sex or chat activities.

Here is a brief summary of the kinds of sexual behavior that might be expected during various stages of development:

Ages Birth through Five Years: Children like to take off their clothes during their early years. In addition, they often are observed touching their genitals. Many children engage in self-stimulating behavior or masturbation, even at early ages. Masturbation can reduce tension and provide pleasure for young children. Young children are also very curious about their bodies and the bodies of others. They may look at the private parts of other children or adults, and they may try to touch others' private parts. Children age five or younger who are engaging in or simulating vaginal or anal intercourse or any type of oral-genital contact, however, should be assessed by a specialist who evaluates or treats children with sexual behavior problems.

Ages Six through Nine Years: Children this age continue to show interest in their bodies and the bodies of other children. Children may use sexual words or tell sexual jokes that they do not even understand. It is normal for children to play looking or touching games such as "Doctor" or "Truth or Dare." Children of this age who are attempting vaginal or anal penetration or oral sex are probably engaging in sexual behavior outside the norm, though, and they should be assessed by a specialist.

Ages 10 through 12 Years: Many children start masturbating around this time, and an increase in sexual drive and interest can be expected. Increased sexual activity with same-age children is common and consists of touching, kissing, and genital rubbing. Many children engage in these activities with same-sex partners, and it does not indicate that they will eventually identify themselves as gay, lesbian, or bisexual. Same-sex sexual behavior is developmentally normal. Children in this age range who are engaging in sexual behavior with much younger children (more than two or three years younger than themselves) or who are using threats, force, or bribes to accomplish their sexual behavior—regardless of the age or sex of the other child—should be assessed by a specialist.

Ages 13 through 18 Years: Boys and girls have usually started to masturbate by this age, and they do it often. Once a day is not uncommon. What is uncommon is for a child (or adult) to be observed or "caught" masturbating. Most people go through their lives rarely, if ever, being observed masturbating. Adolescents who are regularly seen masturbating may be so compulsive about it that they are oblivious to what is going on around them, or they may be seeking some additional stimulation from having someone see them. Either way, an adolescent with this behavior may need to be assessed by a specialist. Adolescents also start engaging in sexual behaviors such as vaginal intercourse and oral-genital contact (*fellatio* is the word for mouth-to-penis contact; *cunnilingus* describes mouth-to-vagina contact). Concerned adults always hope that good sex education has provided adolescents with

the information they need to take responsibility for birth control and that the youth also get tested to rule out sexually transmitted diseases in themselves and their partners.

Adolescents who touch younger children, force or coerce peers to engage in sexual behavior without concern for preserving the relationship between them, or encourage their potential partners to use drugs or alcohol in order to accomplish sexual contact usually have a sexual behavior problem and need to be assessed by a specialist. Also, adolescents who show an inability to control their impulses—those who make repeated calls to sex talk lines, who call strangers or acquaintances and use sexual talk, or who steal underwear or expose their genitals to others—need to be assessed by a specialist.

Is it true that all children or adolescents with sexual behavior problems have been sexually abused themselves? And if previous abuse is not a factor, what else is?

No, not all children who abuse have themselves been sexually abused. In outpatient treatment programs, as many as half the adolescents have not been sexually abused. Other negative factors, however, can play a role in the development of sexually inappropriate behavior in children and adolescents. Those negative factors include such things as ADHD, the use of drugs or alcohol, poor social skills, exposure to pornography or other sexually stimulating experiences, social alienation, repressive or overly permissive sexual attitudes from parents, home-life instability or neglect, crowded living conditions (such as lack of private bedrooms), or exposure to domestic violence or physical abuse.

In addition, other normal evolutionary factors such as the onset of puberty, frequent or unsupervised access to younger children, and many other situational and developmental factors can motivate sexual exploration that is done abusively—with or without awareness of the damage it inflicts and with or without the intent to do harm. Peer pressure or inexperience can also sometimes contribute to abusive sexual behaviors such as date rape.

Research has shown that children develop sexual behavior problems for many different reasons. In addition to the factors listed above, the quality of supervision and the presence of vulnerable people (that is, potential victims) are important situational factors. In recent years, the Internet has brought a tremendous amount of sexual information, sexual talk, and easily accessible pornography to the fingertips, eyes, and minds of millions of children and adolescents.

According to current statistics, adolescent girls who engage in sexually abusive behavior are more likely to have a history of being sexually abused than are adolescent boys. Your child's therapist will work hard to determine whether any sexual abuse has played a part in your child's history. If you suspect that abuse has occurred, it is very important to share that information with your child's evaluator or treatment provider.

In most treatment programs, your child will learn that his or her behavior involved a personal choice. Many treatment programs emphasize personal responsibility for all behavior choices. In this sense, your child will learn that no "cure" exists for sexual acting-out because no cure exists for poor decision making. No cure is possible because such actions are not the result of a disease; they are the result of a personal choice. Successful treatment for sexual behavior problems requires that youths become responsible individuals in all aspects of their day-to-day lives.

In summary, children and adolescents with sexual behavior problems are a mixed group, with no single cause for their sexual acting-out. A typical outpatient treatment program contains a cross section of society, including good students and below-average students, athletic and nonathletic youths, religious and nonreligious kids, high-functioning and lower functioning participants, and both males and females.

In what settings are children and adolescents with sexual behavior problems treated?

Children with sexual behavior problems can be treated on an outpatient basis if they are in a stable living situation that provides adequate controls and supervision. If a youth's sexual behavior is violent, or if the child's parent or guardian feels unable to control the youth or protect an in-home victim, residential or institutional treatment or placement in a home without other younger children may be indicated. It is important that parents find a counselor in or near their communities who specializes in evaluating and treating children or adolescents with these specific types of problems.

How successful is treatment for children and adolescents with sexual behavior problems?

Recidivism is the term for reoffending, and the recidivism rate is one measure of how successful a treatment program has been. Few studies of children and adolescents in treatment have gone beyond five years in researching recidivism. Several studies show sexual reoffense rates as low as 8–15 percent over a five-year period for children and adolescents without a serious history of delinquency or conduct disorder. A 2010 study involving over 11,000 juvenile sex offenders found that the base rate for sexual reoffense is 7.08 percent.[*] For adolescents with delinquent behavior patterns, up to 50 percent continue to have problems with delinquent behavior, although it doesn't always include sexual reoffenses. As previously stated, it is very clear that most children and adolescents with sexual behavior problems do not grow up to continue their sexually abusive behaviors. With effective treatment and good supervision, most children and adolescents with sexual behavior problems can remain in their communities and live successful lives.

---

[*] Michael Caldwell, "Study Characteristics and Recidivism Base Rates in Juvenile Sex Offender Recidivism," *International Journal of Offender Therapy and Comparative Criminology* 54, no. 2 (April 2010): 197–212.

Our religion discourages masturbation. Will my child be required to masturbate as part of treatment?

Some parents have very strong feelings about masturbation, which may stem from their own family or religious upbringing. Some well-known and respected religions such as Jehovah's Witnesses and the Church of Latter Day Saints (Mormons) very much discourage masturbatory behavior. Most good treatment programs will encourage clients to talk about their masturbatory practices and beliefs during the treatment process, but very few, if any, treatment programs will require clients to masturbate. Most therapists want their clients to be honest about their masturbatory behavior, and many therapists will talk with clients about how to have healthy and legal masturbatory behavior. It is important that parents talk openly with their child's therapist about their cultural or religious beliefs, so that the therapist can develop a treatment plan that is sensitive to the needs of each family.

How is success defined in the treatment of children and adolescents with sexual behavior problems?

Successful treatment means that the child performs no additional acts of aggressive or illegal sexual behavior for the duration of his or her life. In 1993, a national task group developed standards of practice for adolescent sex offenders and came up with a list of progress indicators. Those indicators still have value today. The list that follows is based on those indicators.

Treatment Progress Indicators for Adolescents with Sexual Behavior Problems

A teen's treatment progress, or lack of progress, is evaluated by looking at whether he or she has achieved certain measurable goals and objectives, is cooperative in treatment, maintains control of and responsibility for his or her own thoughts

and actions, changes his or her abuse-supporting patterns of thinking, and makes changes in behavior that therapists and parents or guardians can see over time.

An adolescent shows treatment progress when he or she:

1. Accepts responsibility for the inappropriate or illegal sexual behavior without denying that he or she did it, minimizing any part of the behavior, or blaming the victim, the system, or anyone else;
2. Shows, by his or her behavior, positive steps toward reaching treatment goals;
3. Shows that he or she can identify the factors that contributed to the previous abusive patterns (also known as an "offending cycle");
4. Makes positive changes in these contributing factors or is working on resolving these issues;
5. Learns how his or her behavior hurt the victims (empathy) and demonstrates empathy in thinking about the effects of his or her actions on others;
6. Can handle emotional stress in nonhurtful ways and has learned how to change negative feelings;
7. Has learned to feel better about himself or herself;
8. Reports fantasies and interactions that show responsible, consenting sexuality involving same-age partners;
9. Gets involved in positive, nonsexual social activities with other adolescents who are positive role models. Those role models can include teens who have good study or work habits or those who can have fun without drinking or taking drugs;
10. Has good relationships and interactions with family members;
11. Is open and sharing when looking at his or her own thoughts, fantasies, and behaviors;

12. Can reduce and control his or her sexual arousal toward potential victims in fantasies or in social or family situations;

13. Has fewer fantasies involving victims and nonconsenting sex and, at the same time, has built up more fantasies that involve healthy, nonabusive, consenting sexual relationships with partners of a similar age and ability;

14. Can understand and reason against his or her own irrational thinking (thinking errors—please see pages 45–48) and those of others;

15. Is able to interrupt his or her abusive pattern or cycle and get help when a destructive or risky behavior pattern begins;

16. Can speak up for himself or herself in an assertive way and communicate feelings and thoughts to others;

17. Has done some emotional work to resolve any issues about being a victim of abuse in the past or about experiencing a death or separation among family members or close friends;

18. Can experience pleasure in normal activities;

19. Can understand and communicate the new behavior patterns he or she is learning in treatment and transfer them to behavior in the home and community; and

20. Has helped family (or support team) members learn to recognize the risk factors in the offending cycle, has learned how to aid himself or herself to manage those factors differently, or has learned how to get help.

There is a treatment progress scale for adolescents with sexual behavior problems called the Treatment Planning and Progress Inventory for Youths Who Sexually Abuse.* That progress scale measures nine dimensions of a youth's behavior in order to arrive at an assessment of treatment progress.

1. Inappropriate sexual behavior (9 items): the extent to which the adolescent displays inappropriate sexuality, shows deviant sexual interests, and is preoccupied with sexual matters.

2. Healthy sexuality (10 items): the extent to which the adolescent demonstrates an understanding and expression of healthy sexual behavior.

3. Social competency (8 items): the extent to which the adolescent shows appropriate social skills and has healthy social connections.

4. Cognitions supportive of sexual abuse (6 items): the extent to which the adolescent uses cognitions supportive of sexual abuse.

5. Attitudes supportive of sexual abuse (6 items): the extent to which the adolescent endorses attitudes supportive of sexual abuse.

6. Victim awareness (4 items): the extent to which the adolescent understands that he/she harmed the victim(s) of the sexual abuse.

7. Affective/behavioral regulation (8 items): the extent to which the adolescent is able to manage nonsexual and sexual impulses and to learn from consequences of behavior.

8. Risk prevention awareness (7 items): the extent to which the adolescent knows how to prevent additional sexual offenses.

9. Positive family caregiver dynamics (6 items): the extent to which the family

---

* Brent J. Oneal, G. Leonard Burns, Timothy J. Kahn, Phil Rich, and James R. Worling, "Initial Psychometric Properties of a Treatment Planning and Progress Inventory for Adolescents Who Sexually Abuse," *Sexual Abuse* 20 (2008): 161.

caregivers appreciate factors related to the sexual abuse, practice appropriate parenting strategies, and demonstrate a quality of interactions between the adolescent and family caregivers.

Treatment Progress Indicators for Younger Children with Sexual Behavior Problems

Lucy Berliner, M.S.W., from the Harborview Center for Traumatic Stress in Seattle has described some basic but appropriate treatment goals for preteen children with sexual behavior problems. Berliner's treatment goals for children with sexual behavior problems are as follows.

Treatment Goals for Children with Sexual Behavior Problems (Ages 6 to 12)

1. Child has accurate sexual knowledge.
2. Child has rules for healthy sexual behavior.
3. Child can talk about the sexual behavior he or she has done.
4. Child has an accurate understanding of his or her responsibility in the situation.
5. Child can identify the distorted thinking that was involved in the behavior.
6. Child has a plan of what he or she is going to do when the urge to repeat the behavior occurs again.
7. Child knows where to turn for help.
8. Child has skills to use in case abusive thoughts occur.
9. Child's family supervises the child effectively and closely monitors contact with other children.
10. The family environment is decreasing the probability of the behavior occurring.
11. The boundaries and the behavior of other family members are appropriate.

Is there anything about my child that might suggest that he or she will succeed or fail in treatment?

Many factors help predict the relative success of the treatment process for an individual child or teen. Clearly, the longer and more frequently he or she has either been abused or has been acting out sexually, the more difficult treatment tends to be. Children as young as 10 years old may have been acting out sexually for three or four years. Another relevant factor is whether the child has other behavior problems and how serious or disruptive those behaviors are. The more "conduct disordered" a youth is, the more difficult the treatment process becomes. Conduct-disordered youth break laws and rules, lie and cheat, and do things to damage property or other people. Another significant factor is how stable or unstable the child's living environment is. It is often difficult for children with sexual behavior problems who are in foster homes, group homes, or other residential facilities to establish long-term attachments and relationships. This factor complicates treatment by making it hard to build a sense of trust in treatment and in other relationships.

How long does treatment last?

It depends to a large extent on how long your child's sexual behavior problems have been occurring, how ingrained and compulsive the behavior is, and how intensive the treatment program is. When a child's parents are supportive, involved in treatment, and committed to providing appropriate supervision, the treatment process can be shorter than it otherwise would be. As a general rule, 18 months is a reasonable average for weekly outpatient therapy; six months is often considered the absolute minimum. Some adolescents with long histories of sexual acting-out may require at least three years or more of specialized counseling or intensive treatment in a residential facility. Some young children with active, healthy family systems may require only a few weeks or months of actual counseling, coupled with close supervision and support from their parents and other caregivers. It is important to understand that treatment is not considered "completed" in a residential facility. Residential group homes and institutions are artificial environments with high levels of structure and supervision. Many youth do well in such facilities, only to regress when they move home to less structured living situations.

One other essential factor plays a role in the treatment of a sexually misbehaving young child: the onset of puberty. For example, if a nine-year-old boy sexually acts out with a five-year-old, the nine-year-old will generally start the treatment process fairly quickly and may be ready to graduate from treatment when he is 10 or 11. But 10- or 11-year-olds rarely understand the intensity of the sexual feelings they will experience when they start puberty. Those new feelings and that intensity can reactivate the old patterns of thinking and feeling that got them into treatment in the first place. So it is very important to discuss this issue with your child's treatment provider. Experience has taught us that terminating therapy just before puberty is often not in the child's best interest. Maintaining some periodic therapeutic contact through the first year or two of puberty is often a good idea.

You can encourage your child at any age to take responsibility for his or her own treatment. Tell him or her that the length of treatment depends to a large extent on how hard he or she works in therapy, the quality of his or her homework assignments, the level of participation in group and individual sessions, and his or her willingness and ability to apply what is being learned in treatment to situations in daily life.

How do I talk with my child about his or her sexual behavior problems?

You've made a good start by reading this parents' guide, and you also may have read your child's treatment workbook or treatment program outline. If your child is not using a workbook, ask your child's evaluator or treatment provider for copies of the materials that are being used in the treatment process. If your child is in a residential or institutional treatment program, talk with the staff there to find out about the rules and guidelines in that program. If you are still unsure about how to talk with your child, consider asking your child's counselor for help. Sometimes sitting in on a session with your child and the counselor will give you ideas about how to talk about difficult-to-share issues such as sexual abuse and sexuality in general. The best strategy is to be direct and forthright. As your child progresses in counseling, and as you become more comfortable with sexual discussions, you may get the okay from your child's counselor (and your child) to review parts of your child's treatment book. By keeping communications open with both your child and the counselor, you increase the chances that your child will come to you to discuss feelings and urges in the future, before serious problems recur.

Many parents and other relatives are hesitant to ask a child questions about his or her treatment process due to fear of causing embarrassment or shame. Many years of experience has found that it is very helpful for parents and supportive relatives to ask a child direct questions about the treatment process. This gives the youth a chance to review what is being learned in treatment, and it also helps build a more open parent-child relationship.

What if my child denies doing the sexual behavior for which he or she is accused?

First, don't be surprised. Most children and adolescents initially deny the full extent of their sexual behavior, especially when talking with their parents. In time, with counseling and support for telling the truth, most youth make gradual progress toward disclosing the full extent of their abusive behavior. The best thing you can do is listen carefully to your child's story, note any inconsistencies, and reassure your child that if his or her story changes at a later date, it is okay to tell you. Even though you will have a very hard time discovering that the child you have raised and loved is a sexual offender or a child with sexual behavior problems, never support your child's denial by agreeing that he or she could not have engaged in the sexual misbehavior. Even if you have your own doubts about what happened, be neutral and open to the possibility that anything might have happened, and avoid showing support for or belief in your child's explanations and excuses.

When your child completely denies all sexual misconduct, the next step is to talk with your child's counselor so that a plan can be developed to help get to the truth. Because denial often comes across as either a deliberate lie or a lack of remorse for hurting someone, it is better to help your child get through the denial stage before an official investigation begins. If your child can get through denial before going to court, it is more likely that a judge will see your child as someone who can be salvaged with the right kind of help and supervision rather than as someone who needs to be punished.

Won't I make my child's problems worse by continuing to bring them up?

No. You actually can make those problems worse by ignoring or avoiding them. It is true that your child may be uncomfortable talking about what he or she has done. Later on, however, that same discomfort may be a helpful reminder that sexual acting-out or sexual offending is not worth the consequences of having to face up to one's actions. Proactively talking with your child about his or her behaviors and helping your child throughout his or her treatment are the two best ways to help your child discontinue sexual acting-out.

Secrecy plays a major part in how sexual abuse happens and how long it continues. Whatever your child tells you about his or her thoughts, feelings, and behavior should be shared with your child's treatment provider. The goal is to eventually learn the whole extent of what your child has done and what thoughts, feelings, and actions led to the hurtful behavior. You and your child should avoid secrecy at all costs. As parents, you need to learn about all the elements of the treatment process.

Parents are often uncomfortable with sexual topics and don't know what to say to their children about sexual behavior, either the children's or their own. At the end of this book, you will find a list of questions appropriate for your child as he or she moves through the treatment process in *Roadmaps* or *Pathways*. You would be well advised to ask your child those questions. If your child is using other treatment workbooks or materials, get familiar with those publications and ask questions that support the learning processes described in those books. It is essential that you get involved in your child's treatment and stay involved. Some treatment programs have support and education groups for parents. Ask your child's treatment provider if such a group exists in your area. If so, get involved in that group. Even if a group is not available, talk often with your child's treatment provider. Check in with the counselor on a weekly basis, and keep the channels of communication open.

What if my child's behavior isn't as bad as that of other children or adolescents in the treatment program? Will my child be exposed to even worse behaviors or possibly be victimized by others in the program?

Good treatment programs have strict rules about behavior during group therapy sessions. Most children and adolescents who participate in outpatient treatment programs are working hard to learn new skills and get their lives under control. Most treatment groups are supportive places where those youth can get help for all their current life problems and problems that arise in the future.

Good treatment programs do not allow victimizing or abusive behavior to take place during treatment, and poor attitudes about sexuality, drugs, crime, and the like are strongly challenged in treatment programs. If you see behavior in the office or outside the office that concerns you, discuss it with your child's treatment provider so that appropriate action can be taken. Some parents wonder why residential and institutional treatment programs have such strict rules about physical contact, supervision, and even what children can watch on TV. Those rules have been developed over many years to keep these children safe. Children and adolescents in residential and institutional programs often have very severe sexual and mental health problems, and such strict rules help make sure that none of the clients hurt each other or themselves.

Because of concerns about the behavior of these children, in many places it is hard to find office space for such treatment programs. You can help your child's treatment program get along with its neighbors by monitoring and controlling your child's behavior in the counselor's office, by making sure that your child is prepared for each therapy session, and by ensuring that your child is dressed in an appropriate manner.

Should I say anything to my child's teachers or school principal?

Generally, select school personnel should be told about a child's sexual behavior problem if the sexual behavior occurred in a school setting or if the child is so impulsive that school staff need to have the information in order to protect potential victims or other vulnerable people. When a child's sexual behavior problem is chronic (continues despite efforts to stop it), or when a child is very low functioning or requires special supervision in general, it is always a good idea to meet regularly with the school administration or counseling staff to discuss your child's issues and behavior problems.

Children and adolescents with sexual behavior problems have a right to privacy. The general standard is that enough information about those youth needs to be released to ensure that other people are protected and safe. In some states, the juvenile court is required by law to notify school administrators any time an adolescent pleads guilty to or is found guilty of a sexual offense. In those cases, it might be a good idea for parents to meet with school staff before the formal notification occurs. The decisions about whether to talk to school personnel, which staff should receive the information, and what to tell them should be weighed carefully by the youth and his or her parents after talking with the child's treatment provider.

My child has molested another child of the same gender. Does that mean my child is gay or lesbian?

No. Years of research and experience have found that many children who act out sexually with other children of the same gender end up living completely heterosexual lives. Many nonoffending adults have had sexual experiences with people of the same gender when growing up, and most of them do not end up gay or lesbian. Children and adolescents often experience sexual feelings toward the same gender, or even animals, and as they mature their sexual preferences become more stable, with most of them becoming heterosexual. It is important to note, however, that some children and adolescents with or without sexual behavior problems will discover during their adolescence that they are gay, lesbian, or bisexual (attracted to both genders). Parents should be open to that possibility and realize that most gay and lesbian people live happy, crime-free lives.

When will I be able to trust my child around other children again?

The safest answer—though not the one you want to hear—is probably not for a long time. This answer recognizes that preventing your child from being alone with other children is a very important external barrier to further sexual misconduct or sexual offenses. The issue here is trust. Children and adolescents with sexual behavior problems need better-than-average supervision. Many such children have wonderful intentions but very poor impulse control. In those instances, the issue of trust is not the only influencing factor. Your child will likely be able to live with other children, but he or she will require much closer supervision than other children.

Many states and countries have implemented sex offender registration and notification processes. Some teenagers do commit very heinous crimes. Thanks to research, however, we have a more sophisticated and accurate understanding of risk factors now, although our understanding of those factors is still not perfect. Your child may be considered a potentially dangerous person, even though your experience of your own child is as an innocent and cooperative member of the family. Fortunately, as this book stresses over and over, the vast majority of young people with sexual behavior problems are good people at heart, and they will be able to overcome their sexual misconduct and go on to live healthy and productive lives.

Children and their parents must understand, however, that reoffenses and further sexual behavior problems are always possible. The thoughts and feelings that led to the initial sexual acting-out will almost certainly come back. It's how your child deals with those feelings that makes the difference between an abuse-free future or a future of reoffending. The more you— as a concerned, involved parent—and your child can build and maintain barriers to offending, the lower your child's chances will be of acting out sexually again. Please refer to the accompanying diagram on page 29 to understand the four preconditions for sexual abuse.

In many treatment programs, participants learn that a key part of any treatment process is to build up the barriers that protect against further sexual acting-out. Those barriers may include restrictions about certain activities, but they also may contain positive protective factors.

Building up just one barrier is not enough. Think for a moment about a teenage boy who committed a very serious sexual offense against a young girl in his apartment complex after getting sentenced for a different sexual offense. If he had been more honest about his feelings in treatment, perhaps he would have shared his inap-

propriate thoughts or urges with his treatment group and therapist. Then additional treatment activities might have helped him get his urges under control. Controlling offending fantasies and urges is part of building up the motivation barrier. If the probation officer or therapist had visited the apartment complex and noticed that younger children were playing nearby, that adult might have ordered stronger rules for restricting the boy's access to young children. The adult also could have put better supervision in place to help build up external barriers that might have prevented the boy's reoffense.

The following illustration provides a framework for the assessment and treatment process.* The clients discover why their four barriers were not stronger before they acted out sexually. They learn how they can build up those barriers as high as possible, and how and why they need to kick away the "ladders" and "stairs" and unplug the "drill" they used in the past to get through the barriers. When both parents and children learn and practice these skills, it helps tremendously to create an environment that prevents future sexual acting-out.

Please don't make the mistake that other parents of teens with sexual behavior problems have made. Too many parents ask their teenager to babysit after the teen's active treatment work has concluded, to demonstrate trust in their child. Sometimes those parents think this step will prove once and for all—to them and to others—that their child's problems have been cured. Unfortunately, this type of action actually frequently encourages a child to reoffend and provides the child with the opportunity to do so.

It may help to remember that some elements of sexual acting-out can be similar to addictive behaviors such as alcoholism or eating disorders. Supportive friends and relatives of recovering alcoholics do not take the alcoholics into bars to test their strength of will or to show trust. Even alcoholics who have not taken a drink for 20 years

---

* Based on material in D. Finkelhor, *Child Sexual Abuse: New Theory and Research* (New York: Free Press, 1984), 53–68.

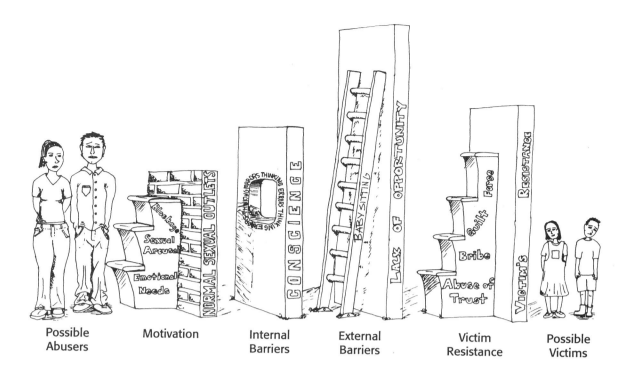

Possible Abusers   Motivation   Internal Barriers   External Barriers   Victim Resistance   Possible Victims

still consider themselves alcoholics. They control their behavior by choosing every single day not to drink. Alcoholics cannot be cured, but they can control their behavior with help and support and with shaping their actions to protect themselves from situations that could weaken their resolve.

People with sexual problems need to develop a similar attitude, although the control of sexual urges is actually more like dieting. Dieting involves controlling an urge (eating) that is very similar to the sexual urge, in that both are instinctual and both are a key part of the human existence. We know through research and experience that fad diets do not work and that losing weight permanently requires making major lifestyle changes with a lot of environmental support. Healthy control of sexual feelings also requires that a person learns and maintains healthy sexual values and attitudes, while surrounded by a network of people who provide ongoing support.

Will my child grow up to become an adult sex offender?

As you have learned, little long-term follow-up research has been conducted about children and adolescents with sexual behavior problems. Research done so far, however, seems to indicate that the reoffense (recidivism) rate for juveniles who commit sexual offenses is significantly lower than that for adults.[*]

Reoffense rates are even lower for adolescents who successfully complete treatment programs that are targeted on sexual behavior issues. It is generally agreed by officials, researchers, and therapists that when strong, specialized treatment programs are provided for children and adolescents with sexual behavior problems, communities and families will be safer and will experience fewer cases of sexual reoffending.

How can I support my child's treatment process?

To begin, you should review your child's treatment workbook or treatment handouts before your child writes in them. If your child is not using a treatment workbook, ask the counselor for

---

[*] Chaffin, Bonner, and Pierce, *Fact Sheet: What Research Shows About Adolescent Sex Offenders* (July 2003), www.ncsby.org.

whatever information is available about the treatment program he or she will be giving your child. Read that material and ask questions so that you understand what is expected of your child during treatment.

Certain assignments in treatment workbooks and handouts, however, are private and may not be shared with parents until a child is ready to share them. Once your child has started working on a workbook or treatment handouts, it is important that you respect your child's privacy and look only at the parts he or she has agreed to share with you. Essentially, your child's treatment work becomes a boundary; you can support this aspect of treatment by fully respecting your child's boundary.

But that doesn't mean you will not be aware of what your child is working on in treatment. One of the purposes of this parents' guide is to provide you with two lists of questions that you may ask as your child completes each chapter in the *Pathways* or *Roadmaps* workbook. As your child completes each chapter, you should make the time to sit down with the child and ask those questions. By remaining aware of your child's treatment work and by asking questions about what he or she is learning, you, too, will learn about sexual abuse treatment and your child's progress—and your child will know that you care about how he or she is doing. If your child is not working in *Roadmaps* or *Pathways*, you should still ask your child and your child's counselor if you can become familiar with what your child is learning. Most counselors welcome a parent's involvement in the counseling process so that skills learned in the counselor's office can be supported and practiced at home.

Although your involvement in the treatment process is a good thing, many parents have difficulty resisting the temptation to look at their child's treatment work without permission. This temptation is normal, but to secretly look at your child's work is a serious boundary violation. Your child has been learning (or will learn) to respect the boundaries of others, which will, in turn, make

a recurrence of his or her sexual acting-out less likely. It is essential, therefore, that you demonstrate an equal respect for your child's boundaries. As the parent, your job is to model this behavior. In respecting the boundaries around your child's treatment work, you demonstrate respect and consideration for your child.

You may have other questions that haven't been answered here. Ask those questions of your child's evaluator or treatment provider. Most will welcome your interest and will help you find the correct answers for your child's situation.

What can I do if my child is in a residential or institutional treatment facility?

If your child is placed out of your home and into a residential or institutional facility, there are some things you can do to support your child's effective treatment. Some of those things are:

- Arrive on time for scheduled visits. When parents are late, children and adolescents often feel frustrated and disappointed, which can lead to behavior problems in the facility.
- Be consistent, and follow through with your promises. If you have to cancel a visit or miss a phone call, notify the staff at the facility and ask that they notify your child.
- Always check in with staff during your visits. Also check in with staff by phone on a regular basis.
- Ask questions about rules and expectations. Sometimes staff want to handle all discipline during your visits, but at other times staff may expect the parent to do some discipline. Find out what is required in your child's facility!
- Make sure that you supervise and control any other children that you bring to the facility. Don't expect staff to supervise your other children.
- Remember that staff members are usually

well-educated and well-trained. They may, however, be young and just out of college. This is because most residential facilities cannot afford to pay high salaries for experienced counselors. Be aware that those staff members are not trying to take your place as the parent!

Some of the counselors and staff in my child's residential treatment program seem really young. Do they have the skills and experience to provide effective treatment to my child?

This is a very good question; many of the counselors and staff who work in residential and institutional programs *are* very young. In most cases, however, the counselors and staff have at least four years of college training, and even if they are inexperienced, they are generally supervised by older staff who have more experience. Since the staff may be younger, they are often able to establish good, caring relationships with clients, and many clients report that they have developed trusting relationships with those younger staff members.

Consider the comments of the mother of a young adolescent who had acted out sexually:

> This incident with my son's offending has had greater immediate and long-term impacts than many of my other life experiences. Perhaps in a few years, I'll look back and it will be another chapter or growth in my life. I don't know. I hope so. One of the most frightening aspects of this problem is that it seems to have no closure, no ending, and no point at which we will put it behind us.

In most treatment programs, and as we've said earlier in this book, your child will be learning that no "cure" exists for sexual behavior problems, primarily because sexual acting-out is not a disease. Sexual behavior problems involve misguided, self-centered, or impulsive choices that a child or teen can learn to control and change. By paying attention to warning signs, avoiding high-risk situations, making and maintaining lifestyle changes, and making an ongoing commitment to healthy relationships, your child can move away from any future sexual behavior problems. With attention to these issues and a strong support system, control and positive behavioral choices are possible, allowing families to return to a relatively normal life.

As a parent, it is your responsibility to continue to support and monitor your child's efforts to maintain the changes made in treatment. Remember, one of the most effective ways of preventing future sexual behavior problems is to set up external barriers that limit your child's unsupervised contact with potential victims. With treatment successfully completed and with continued attention to your child's aftercare or relapse prevention plan, you can know that your child's future holds the possibility of healthy and productive relationships.

12 Steps for Parents

The following set of concepts has been adapted from the 12-step program of Alcoholics Anonymous. It might just save your sanity when your life is full of the stress of dealing with the changes in your family and with the legal and treatment professionals who are involved in much of what you do now. The following 12 steps for parents will help to provide some structure for what can seem like a never-ending process. These 12 steps are a helpful way of looking at how you can support and enhance the treatment process for your child. This list may give you some ideas about how you can adopt positive, healthy attitudes about your child's behavior and treatment.[*]

---

[*] Adapted from K. MacFarlane and C. Cunningham, *Steps to Healthy Touching* (1988). Reprinted with permission of KIDSRIGHTS.

12 Steps for Parents

1. I acknowledge that my child has been involved in some inappropriate sexual behavior and that the problem is too big for me or my family to handle alone.

2. I believe that there are people who care about my child and my family who can help us with this problem. (I also believe that a power greater than ourselves can help us if we are open to receiving it.)

3. I have decided to allow people who understand this problem to help my family get control over it.

4. I will stop blaming other people or the "system" for my family's problem and admit how serious this problem has become.

5. I admit to myself and to other people (and to my higher power) exactly what my child has done that is wrong and harmful to others. I also acknowledge the possibility that I may have unknowingly contributed to my child's inappropriate behavior.

6. I am ready to do whatever is necessary to help my child change his or her behavior. I am willing to examine my own behaviors, attitudes, and feelings so that my family can find better ways to communicate feelings.

7. I am willing to examine my own history of victimization and abusive or addictive behaviors so that my personal issues will not hinder me from helping my child with his or hers.

8. I recognize that there are things about myself and my family that I can change and other things that I cannot change. Beginning with my own faults, I am working on changing the things I can.

9. I am learning to recognize the signs and situations that mean that my child may be at risk of further abusive behavior. I am willing to ask for help when I recognize these warning signals.

10. I am ready to acknowledge the harm that my child's behavior has caused, and I am willing to help my child make amends whenever that is possible.

11. I will continue to be aware of my child's problem, and I will not respond with impatience or feelings of false security. I recognize that my child needs my help, and I will take necessary precautions to help prevent the victimization of other children.

12. I will help other parents of children who have this problem by sharing my feelings and experiences and by helping them see that they and their children need help.

Chapter 4

Understanding the Assessment Process

Assessment (also called *evaluation*) is the process of finding out what the problem is and then recommending what to do about it. When the problem is inappropriate or illegal sexual behavior by a child, the person doing the assessment talks with the child, his or her family members, representatives of child protective services, and perhaps some other people who are involved with the family. The assessment professional (evaluator) also reviews victim statements or talks to other professionals who have information about what the victim reported happening. The evaluator tries to get a complete picture of what happened and why, before suggesting a course of action to prevent it from happening again. The child's thoughts, feelings, and behaviors are assessed. The evaluator tries to determine how stable the child's family environment is, and whether anyone else knew about or was involved in the abuse. The evaluator also tries to determine whether the child has been emotionally, physically, or sexually abused by anyone in or around the family, and he or she tries to find out whether or not family members can establish and maintain rules about behavior and whether they can provide the very close supervision that is necessary when sexual abuse has occurred.

The assessment process for your child can include both talking and testing. Most of the assessment process involves the evaluator talking with your child to find out about his or her sexual learning experiences. The evaluator will also be asking the parents to fill out a variety of questionnaires in order to gain a better understanding of the child's living environment and the parents' strengths and areas of potential growth. Testing may include psychological and physical

tests, including (for older adolescents) measuring your child's sexual responses (using, for boys, a plethysmograph or a visual reaction time test). Plethysmographs and visual reaction time tests are rarely used on children under the age of 16, however, since sexual response patterns are usually not well established until later in adolescence. The assessment also determines the child's physiological response to lying or to telling the truth (using a polygraph). Polygraphs are never used with children under the age of 12 years.

If you have discovered that one of your children has been involved in sexual behavior with a sibling, a critical assessment will be done on you, as well, to judge whether the sexually abusing child should be allowed to live at home alongside his or her victim. The flowchart that follows provides some rough guidelines about whether you or the child protective services caseworker should seek a placement for the abusing child outside the home.

Generally, it is considered a healthy break for all family members when a child with sexual behavior problems lives out of the home for a period of time. This "time out" allows an in-home victim some time without the abuser present, making it easier to talk about what occurred without feeling pressure to keep things secret. It also allows the offending child to experience the real and immediate consequences of his or her abusive behavior, and it reinforces the importance of immediate involvement in therapy. Possible temporary placements for the offending child might include relatives who do not have young children, church members, close family friends, foster homes, or residential treatment centers. Parents may have to call the local Department of Social Services

Placement Decisions with Sexually Aggressive Youth:
A Decision Process Flow Chart

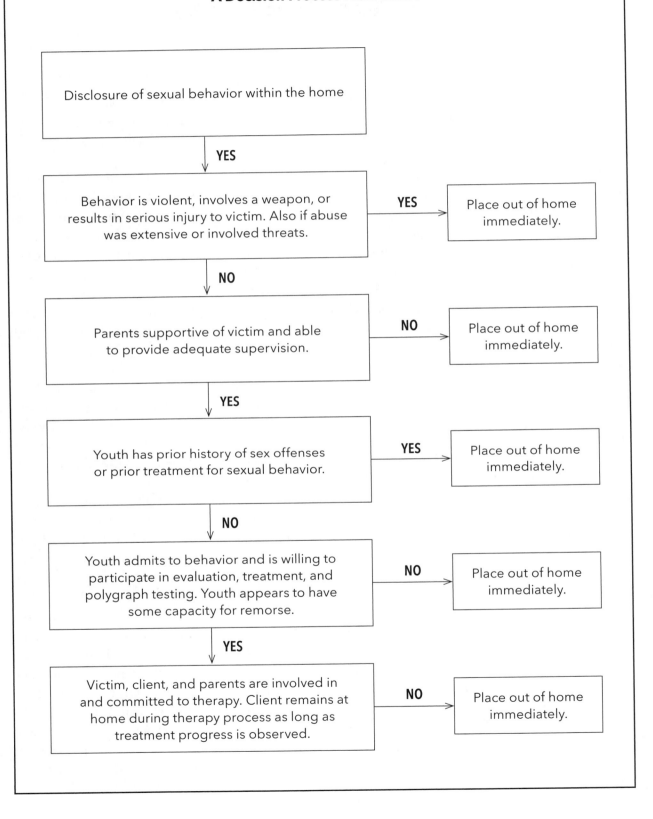

Disclosure of sexual behavior within the home

↓ **YES**

Behavior is violent, involves a weapon, or results in serious injury to victim. Also if abuse was extensive or involved threats. → **YES** → Place out of home immediately.

↓ **NO**

Parents supportive of victim and able to provide adequate supervision. → **NO** → Place out of home immediately.

↓ **YES**

Youth has prior history of sex offenses or prior treatment for sexual behavior. → **YES** → Place out of home immediately.

↓ **NO**

Youth admits to behavior and is willing to participate in evaluation, treatment, and polygraph testing. Youth appears to have some capacity for remorse. → **NO** → Place out of home immediately.

↓ **YES**

Victim, client, and parents are involved in and committed to therapy. Client remains at home during therapy process as long as treatment progress is observed. → **NO** → Place out of home immediately.

to get help in finding a temporary home for their child.

Obviously, whoever is taking care of the child should be fully informed of the child's sexual behavior problems, and no younger or otherwise vulnerable children (with mental or physical handicaps, for example) should live in the new temporary home. It is always a good idea for the child's temporary guardian to meet with the child's counselor to learn about the assessment and treatment process. The new guardian will be responsible for supervising the child most of each day. Therefore, making sure the guardian is educated about the child's supervision needs is very important.

Later in this book you will find guidelines for how to safely arrange for a child's return home, if he or she has been placed out of the home for a period of time. You should not underestimate your own reactions to discovering sexual abuse in your home. One mother of a teenage boy who molested his younger sister decided to let the boy stay in the family home. She agreed to provide the intense supervision needed. After several months of enforcing new supervision and treatment rules, the mother found herself getting more and more angry at her son, and she watched herself rejecting him. Her son then began some self-abusive behavior that was quite serious. After exploring the family dynamics in therapy, the mother disclosed that she had been sexually abused by a teenage boy when she was a little girl and had never really resolved that experience. She found that her hidden anger and resentment were surfacing toward her son in many ways in their daily lives. She was making negative and critical comments, imposing excessively stern discipline, and withholding love and affection. In hindsight, the parents and the teenager all agreed that it would have been far better for all of them if they had arranged out-of-home placement in the first place.

Regardless of what your child's specific sexual problem is, a thorough assessment is generally warranted. By having a thorough assess-

ment done, you can be more confident that your child's sexual behavior will not escalate into more serious difficulties later in life. After your child's sexual acting-out has been reported to the proper authorities (child protective services or law enforcement), a professional assessment is needed to determine what risk he or she presents to others, as well as to determine the factors that contributed to the behavior. A professional assessment helps families, caseworkers, and counselors plan the right treatments. During the assessment process, the professional performing the evaluation looks for information such as that listed below. It is helpful if you call attention to any of these issues in order to make the process go more smoothly and to help the evaluator consider all relevant information.

- How old was your child when you first suspected any sexual acting-out behavior?
- Over what period of time has your child been acting out sexually?
- Has your child abused one child or more than one child? Frequently, it is discovered during the treatment process that other children have also been victims. Parents can support the assessment process by notifying the professional evaluator about any other children who may have been alone with their offending child. For example, the evaluator should be informed of all previous babysitting jobs or younger playmates.
- If the sexual behavior problem involved stealing or taking underwear, making obscene phone calls, or doing exposing behavior, please give a thorough history of all other stealing behavior, harassing phone calls, or other inappropriate sexual behavior (such as masturbating when the client could be seen or the sexual touching of animals).
- If the sexual behavior problem involved the use of force or coercion (such as

threats) to get sexual contact with a younger, same-age, or older victim, it is important to get a history of other aggressive behavior. The evaluator also needs to understand what type of social activities the client is involved in where similar behavior might have occurred.

- If the sexual behavior problem involved the use of drugs or alcohol, a complete summary of all previous incidences of drug and alcohol use (or even suspected use) is very important. It may also be relevant to look at the drinking or drug use of other family members.

- The assessment professional needs to assess what types of intervention and treatment have been tried in the past and determine whether the child returned to the sexual acting-out after the intervention.

- Another factor to determine is whether a known or suspected history of sexual abuse or other inappropriate learning experiences has occurred. Has your child witnessed adult sexual activity, or has he or she had access to any pornographic or sexually explicit materials? Make sure that you tell the evaluator about all incidents of your child accessing pornography on television or on the Internet. Note: If you have Internet access in your home, and you do not know how to check the history of the Internet browser, ask your child's treatment provider for guidance about how to check for inappropriate use. Make sure you tell your child's evaluator about any pornography you may have had hidden in your bedroom or elsewhere in the home.

- What type of mental health treatment has been attempted for your child in the past?

- Is your child on any medications currently, or has he or she been on any medications in the past?

- Do your child's questions or behaviors during play suggest that he or she is preoccupied with sexual behavior or sexual interests?

- Does anybody else in the family or extended family have a history of sexual behavior problems?

- What learning deficits or school problems does your child have? It is very helpful if you provide copies of your child's school and counseling records for your child's evaluator. If your child has an IEP (Individualized Education Plan), it is very helpful to provide the evaluator with a copy of that document.

- What, if any, other delinquent or criminal behavior has your child been involved in (stealing, setting fires, spray painting graffiti, joyriding, or fighting, to name a few examples)?

- Think about your child's daily schedule and activities. Does he or she have any major periods of unscheduled or unsupervised time? During unsupervised time, does he or she have any access to potential victims or to people who might take advantage of him or her?

- Does your child have a history of breaking rules and violating normal expectations, such as not coming home when expected, playing where he or she was told not to play, or spending time with certain friends after being told not to associate with them?

- Does your child have a history of hurting himself or herself or of being mean or cruel to animals?

- Who else visits the home on a regular basis? Do you have other children who sometimes spend time at your home? The presence of other children in your home is very important for the evaluator to know about at the beginning of the assessment process.

These are examples of the type of information a professional evaluator will be seeking from you and your child. The more information you volunteer along these lines, the more accurate and helpful the assessment will be.

Evaluators will be looking at the following factors when determining whether your child has a sexual behavior problem:

- Differences in power between the victim and client, including age, size, and physical and mental ability.
- Intimidation factors, such as a status difference (popular versus unpopular) or the misuse of authority between the victim and the client.
- Manipulation factors, such as verbal coercion, games, tricks, bribes, and promises. These factors relate to how the client got the victim to go along with the sexual behavior.
- Secrecy factors, such as covering up, demanding silence, or using threats.
- Mental health factors, such as past history of mental health treatment, use of psychotropic medications, and psychiatric hospitalization history.
- Family dynamics such as quality of supervision, parenting factors, access to victims, and general family stability issues.
- Obsessive behavior factors related to sexuality. Is your child preoccupied with sexual thoughts or issues?
- Compulsiveness factors. Does your child demonstrate a lack of control over behavior? Is there an "out-of-control" quality to the behavior, or is your child unable to discontinue the behavior after being confronted?
- Sexual abuse and sexual behavior history. All of your child's past abuse experiences and past sexual behavior experiences will be closely evaluated.
- Sexual knowledge and attitudes. Your child's knowledge of sexuality will be assessed, as well as his or her attitudes and beliefs about sexual abuse.
- Legal issues. Sometimes a child engages in sexual behavior that is not forceful or coercive, but the age difference makes the behavior illegal in some places.

It is very helpful if you can call the evaluator's attention to any of these issues, because the more information the evaluator has, the better the treatment plan will be.

The evaluator may also ask you about your own childhood experiences in order to understand more about the family's history. Many parents feel uncomfortable disclosing personal information about their own history or that of other family members. Remember that the evaluator is trying to develop an effective treatment plan for your child, so providing an understanding of your life experiences will help the evaluator to better understand your child's behavior, and your background as a parent. If you are uncomfortable sharing information about your personal history with the evaluator, make sure that you discuss that concern directly with the evaluator. It is helpful when parents volunteer information about other victims or perpetrators of abuse within the extended family. It is also helpful when parents volunteer information about their own personal experiences with sexual abuse.

Managing Environmental Risks

Environmental risks are the places or situations where your child might be exposed to possible victims in your home, a relative's home, the apartment complex, or the neighborhood. As your child goes through the evaluation and risk-assessment process, you (and/or your spouse), other family members, and the evaluator need to work together to provide the right level of supervision without totally stifling the child's social, physical, and emotional development. Following are some questions you can ask the evaluator to help you determine how to provide the right level of supervision for your involved child or adolescent. It is important to understand that each child's case must be considered individually. Some generic answers are provided below, to educate parents about general principles involved in sexual misconduct. Your child's evaluator and treatment provider can provide case-specific answers that take into consideration your child's history, a risk assessment, and an awareness of any other restrictions such as probation or parole rules.

General questions about sexual conduct that you can ask the evaluator include the following:

Is direct, line-of-sight supervision necessary?

Such close supervision generally helps prevent further acting-out and is usually recommended during assessment and early phases of treatment. This level of supervision is dependent on the age of the client. Most younger children require more supervision than most older children. Such intense supervision is usually reduced gradually based on a youth's progress in treatment and ability to demonstrate positive behavior choices.

Can my child babysit for other children?

Babysitting makes control over and unsupervised access to younger children possible. For this reason, most children and adolescents with sexual behavior problems should not babysit or care for other children. Some counselors may make exceptions for very low-risk clients who have no legal charges, but only after that child has completed treatment and is approaching adulthood.

Is special supervision required at school?

If any of a child's sexual behavior problems have occurred at school, then special supervision is often recommended. With young children with sexual behavior problems, bathroom breaks, recess, lunch, school busses, and P.E. classes provide the greatest opportunity for sexual acting-out to occur, and special supervision is often recommended during those activities.

Can our child be home alone when we parents are gone? If so, for how long?

Generally children under age 12 should not be left alone in any home. Some older children can sometimes be left alone at home, based on their risk assessment and probation or parole rules. Parents need to understand that clients sometimes like to be home alone so that they can watch pornographic movies or view pornography online. Such decisions need to carefully consider the child's age, risk assessment, access to such materials, and overall maturity.

Should we tell our neighbors?

Most of the time, neighbors and casual acquaintances are not told about a child's sexual behavior history. An exception to this policy is when parents want to build a better support network of adult supervisors, or when their child is a sexual offender and a community notification effort is pending by law enforcement. In those cases, neighbors often appreciate hearing directly from the parents of the adolescent sex offender about the child's problems, rather than from the police agencies.

Can our child play in the neighborhood with other children?

Again, the decision for this issue needs to be based on a risk-assessment study of the child, but children and adolescents with sexual behavior problems are not only capable of sexual acting-out, they are often more likely to be victimized or taken advantage of by others. Supervised play is often a good thing, whereas unsupervised play can lead to further inappropriate behavior and accusations of neglect against a parent. The adult who supervises the play time should have a good understanding of the child's problem behavior history, and should also be a responsible person.

Can our child go to a friend's house to play? Can our child do overnights at a friend's?

Overnight stays are often more risky than daytime play. Parents need to ask themselves if they would want to have a child with a sexual behavior problem come over to their house. Generally, a parent needs to make sure that no younger or vulnerable children are at the other child's house. The parent should visit the other child's house to get a sense of what happens there. A parent also needs to make sure that another adult is present. The parent of the child with the sexual behavior problem should carefully consider telling the parent of the other child about his or her child's need for extra supervision. Constructive social activities are positive and helpful to children with sexual behavior problems, if the activities are properly supervised.

Can our child have friends over to play? Can those friends stay overnight?

When parents have another child visit their home, it is often preferable to having their child go to another home, because they are fully aware of their own child's history and are probably highly motivated to provide quality supervision of all the children in their home. It is important for parents to understand that most other parents are not accustomed to providing the high level of supervision that a child or adolescent with a sexual behavior problem requires. Therefore, having visits at the client's parents' home is usually the best idea.

Can our child go to Scout meetings or outings?

Although Scouts and other activity meetings are usually supervised, parents need to make sure that enough supervision is provided, based on their child's risk assessment. Outings often have a lower level of supervision, so a parent needs to play it safe and volunteer to go along as a chaperone. This type of preventive effort often keeps children and adolescents—a parent's own child as well as other children—out of trouble.

Can our child go to parks or playgrounds alone?

Most treatment programs will discourage this activity, due to the potential for engaging with younger children or older children. Remember, children with sexual behavior problems are not only more likely to act out themselves; they are also more likely to be victimized by others. This decision also depends on the client's overall risk assessment.

Should our child take the bus to school?

Some children are transported to school on Special Education busses with only a few other children. Many children can handle public bus rides on bigger busses with little difficulty, but any decision about such an activity needs to be made with the child's evaluator or treatment provider. Parents also need to consider walking to and from the bus stop with their child, because problems are just as likely to occur before a child gets on the bus or after he or she gets off.

Should our child walk to school alone?

Walking to school or riding a bike to school can provide helpful exercise, but a parent needs to consider the distance, the distractions along the way, and his or her child's overall risk assessment.

Should our child date? Should our child's girlfriend or boyfriend be told about the sexual behavior problem?

Most treatment programs will honor and respect parents' general wishes with respect to dating. For example, many parents do not want their children going on solitary dates until the children are 16 years old. Dating is generally viewed as a positive, healthy social activity for children in their teens. Many youth in middle school or junior high, however, say they are "going out," "dating," or "seeing" someone when what they really mean is that they just talk to the other person at school.

Treatment programs may have diverse views about when an adolescent should tell a boyfriend or girlfriend about a history of sexual behavior problem. This level of communication may vary depending on whether the youth is a registered sex offender and what his or her overall risk assessment is. Most counselors require that their youthful offenders inform any partners about their sexual behavior history before sexual contact occurs, in the spirit of supporting honest relationships and informed consent.

Should our child drive? Can he or she drive a car alone? Can he or she drive with a peer or older person in the car?

Driving is a big responsibility and a major expense. It is also a privilege that many adolescents very much anticipate being able to do. Most treatment programs leave driving decisions up to parents, because they have most of the legal responsibility for such an activity. Most treatment programs require their youthful clients to immediately report any accidents or tickets, since such factors may shed some light on the lifestyle those youths are living.

Can our child have a job? If so, what jobs are appropriate?

Jobs for teenagers over age 15 are often recommended and supported by treatment providers. By getting and maintaining a job, those teens learn responsibility and increase their self-esteem. Many treatment providers have suggestions about how teens should deal with the issue of their sexual behavior histories on their job applications. Generally, teens who have a formal criminal history need to disclose it on their applications or commit to discussing it during an interview. Teens with no formal criminal record usually can keep their sexual behavior histories confidential. Most teens with sexual behavior problems should avoid applying for jobs that involve direct contact or caregiving for younger children.

As noted above, all of these questions need to be answered on a case-by-case basis, considering your child's behavior history and his or her progress in treatment. It is very important to ask the child's evaluator these and other questions in order to develop an effective community supervision strategy. Chapter 9 contains a blank Safety and Supervision Plan form that you may wish to discuss with the evaluator to devise effective supervision guidelines as early in the process as possible. But even if the evaluator says that it is impossible to assemble guidelines until the evaluation is complete, remember for a short period, too much supervision is safer for your child and any potential victims in your home or neighborhood than too little supervision.

Common Questions About the Assessment Process

What is a polygraph test?

A polygraph is more commonly known as a lie detector test. A polygraph examiner is trained to ask questions while measuring changes in a client's blood pressure, respiration, and galvanic skin response. Polygraph examinations are used in many parts of the United States with adolescents, but they are not appropriate for children under the age of 12. Very little research using polygraphs with adolescents has been conducted, and essentially no research has been done on polygraph use with younger children.

During a polygraph examination, a trained examiner asks the client many different questions, primarily about his or her sexual history. The examiner then picks several key questions and uses them to explore one or more issues about the child's sexual behavior. After reviewing all the data, the examiner writes a report that gives an opinion about whether the client is perceived as being truthful or whether the client appears to be answering in a deceptive manner.

Polygraph examinations encourage clients to tell the truth about very sensitive and embarrassing topics, including their sexual behavior. Evaluators have found that clients who are given polygraph examinations often disclose far more personal information about their sexual behavior and experiences than do clients who are not required to take polygraph examinations. Many juvenile court systems require that clients take periodic polygraph examinations while on probation or parole to help ensure that they are following all treatment and probation or parole conditions. Although polygraph results may not be admissible in a court hearing, the disclosures made during polygraph examinations are usually quite helpful.

Experience has taught us that clients can sometimes "pass" polygraph examinations even when their responses are dishonest. So even though a client is viewed by the examiner as being honest, a possibility still exists that the client is not telling the whole truth. Conversely, just because a client is viewed by the examiner as being dishonest, that does not prove that the client is actually lying. The experience can be so stressful for some clients that even when they're being honest, their nervousness registers on the polygraph as deception. For this reason, responsible evaluators, treatment providers, and probation and parole officers do not make legal decisions or take action based only on the results of a polygraph exam. Evaluators usually try to get corroborating data, or they may increase supervision when a client is perceived as being deceptive during a polygraph test. Polygraph assessments are especially valuable during risk assessment, because they encourage clients to disclose more information than they otherwise would about their past sexual experiences. The best predictor of future behavior is past behavior, so getting accurate sexual history information is a critical part of this process.

What is a plethysmograph examination?

A plethysmograph is a device that measures changes in the volume or circumference of the penis. For a plethysmograph examination, the client goes to a specially equipped lab where a technician performs the assessment. Prior to the assessment, the client and his parent sign consent forms. The client is then taken to a private room and instructed to sit in a comfortable chair with his clothes on. The examiner leaves the room but communicates with the client through an intercom system. The client unzips his pants and puts a measurement device (usually resembling a small rubber band or thin metal ring) on his own penis. The examiner is in a different room monitoring the equipment. During the assessment, the client is asked to listen to tapes of a person describing various sexual situations that involve people of differing ages and genders, and encounters that utilize different degrees of coercion. In some cases, the client views pictures of people of differing ages, usually in varying states of nudity. The monitoring equipment records all changes in the client's penile circumference, therefore giving an objective measure of his sexual arousal patterns.

This assessment protocol is used primarily for adults with sexual behavior problems. It is sometimes used for adolescents between the ages of 14 and 18, but almost never with children under age 14. A similar physiological measurement device for females exists. It utilizes a different sort of plethysmograph device that measures arousal secretions and blood flow to vaginal tissues, but that device is presently used only for research purposes. Females being evaluated for sexual behavior problems will not be asked to participate in an examination utilizing this device.

It should be noted that other assessment methods are commonly used to assess a client's sexual arousal patterns, including questionnaires, a visual reaction time test called the Abel Screen, and sexual-interest, card-sort tests. The visual reaction time test asks clients to look at pictures of fully clothed people. The test measures how long the client studies each picture. Research based on the visual reaction time test suggests that the longer a person looks at a picture, the more interested he or she is in the age group depicted in the picture. A sexual-interest, card-sort test asks clients to read short descriptions of various sexual behaviors and then to rate the description on some type of scale. This test is a self-report that allows clients to communicate what their sexual interests are.

Will the evaluator spend the whole time talking with my child about sex?

No. A thorough assessment covers all parts of a client's life and includes interviews with other family members and an in-depth look at how the client functions in school, with friends and family, and with others. All sexual behavior is controlled by the brain so a thorough assessment needs to explore the client's mental functioning (also known as *cognitive abilities*), values and attitudes, family dynamics, and many other factors that influence behavior, especially sexual behavior.

What will we learn from the assessment process?

For some children and adolescents, sexual acting-out is their unconscious or subconscious way of coping with other life problems such as depression, loneliness, anxiety, or feelings of loss or grief. Children and adolescents often act out sexually because other life problems are causing them distress. A thorough assessment explores all possible triggers for the sexual behavior problem so that an effective treatment plan can be developed.

Chapter 5

Understanding the Treatment Process

Your child's behavior problems are probably not confined to the sexual arena alone; sexual acting-out is often part of a larger pattern of self-gratifying, impulsive, and hurtful behaviors. In most treatment programs, your child learns that the treatment process is concerned with far more than just his or her sexual behavior. In many cases, a sexual behavior problem is simply another expression of your child's other problem areas. You know your child better than anybody else, and you know a great deal about your child's behavior patterns.

While many different approaches are used to treat children and adolescents with sexual behavior problems, some common themes have emerged that apply to most treatment programs. The information that follows can help you understand what you can do to keep the treatment process alive between counseling sessions and after your child completes a treatment program. In brief, you will learn to help your child to:

- Counteract his or her denial and tell the whole truth about the full extent of his or her sexual behavior problems—this also means helping the child work toward becoming a more responsible, honest, and sensitive person;
- Understand his or her motivations for acting out sexually;
- Identify and change the thinking and behavior patterns that support his or her sexual acting-out;
- Understand the chain of events that precede and accompany sexual acting-out so that you can help him or her develop a treatment plan that really works; and

- Learn new skills for feeling expression and self-control that will help your child learn to better cope with life stressors and help him or her develop healthier relationships.

One of the concepts emphasized in treatment programs is that the client needs to develop a healthy and responsible lifestyle by working to eliminate all criminal, hurtful, and irresponsible behavior of any kind. Your child's counselor and treatment group will help explore the ongoing behavior patterns that are illegal, self-centered, impulsive, and hurtful. Many of the assignments given by counselors are designed to help clients take a close look at all their day-to-day behavior patterns.

General Guidelines for Parents

The following guidelines will help you to be an effective support person for your child as the treatment process starts. One of the most essential elements is improving communication with your child. Good communication between you and your child will, in turn, make your child's treatment far more successful.

1. *Demonstrate interest in your child's treatment.* Ask specific questions when driving your child to and from therapy appointments. Ask your child to show you some of his or her treatment work. If your child is in a residential or institutional facility, call or visit your child regularly, and make sure you also talk with the staff members to get their

feedback on your child's behavior. Then you can support or confront your child's positive and negative behaviors. This helps create unity on the treatment team and your child will recognize both you and the staff as his or her treatment team.

2. *Increase your own comfort level when addressing sexual issues.* Use the proper names for sexual body parts and activities (penis, vagina, anal or oral sex, cunnilingus, fellatio, to name a few). You are a role model for your child. Have no shame when talking appropriately about a penis, breast, or vagina, as long as the conversation is respectful and occurs in a private location.

    Remember, sex is a healthy and joyful activity. None of us would be here today if it were not for sex and the sex drive. We want our children to express their sexual feelings appropriately and to have a lifetime of healthy sexual activities that do no harm to others. We do not want them to think that sexuality itself is bad, dirty, or frightening. We also want our children to understand that healthy sexuality involves responsibility, and that both positive and negative consequences can be associated with sexual activity.

3. *Show respect for physical, emotional, and social boundaries at all times, including your children's.* By modeling proper respect for boundaries of all kinds, you are reinforcing a very important treatment concept. Don't hesitate to say to your child, "Whoa, that's a boundary. Let's not go there." At the same time, don't let boundary claims become an excuse for your child to keep secrets. Respect is the key.

4. *Demonstrate responsible thinking in your own day-to-day life.* Look at the list of thinking errors in this chapter, and learn them. If you find yourself using a thinking error, admit it: "Hey, I think I was using a thinking error there. I'd better stop that." By admitting to your own thinking errors, you are being a positive role model for your child. It sets at good example when parents acknowledge their own thinking errors to their children.

5. *Support the idea that honesty is one of the most important concepts and behaviors in a treatment program.* If clients cannot be honest about their sexual feelings and behaviors, it will be very difficult to safely supervise them in the community. Parents should also support the idea that "if you can't talk about it, you shouldn't be doing it." This policy will support the general goal of clients maintaining complete honesty through their treatment process.

6. *Emphasize positive reinforcement with your children.* Be observant so that you catch your children doing things right, and then praise them for it. Remember that low self-esteem is a contributing factor in many sexual behavior problems, so increasing a child's self-esteem is a critical treatment goal. At the same time, don't overpraise. An adolescent may feel patronized when praised for something he or she has been doing well since age six.

7. *Be willing to work on general family and marital issues.* It is important to understand that sometimes sexual behavior problems develop as a result of other dysfunctional or problematic family dynamics. Sometimes parents and other family members need to take a close look at the overall family environment, how parents treat each other, how parents treat their children, and how siblings interact with one another.

Key Concepts

Treatment programs use many different approaches when working with children who have sexual behavior problems. Those approaches include helping children to express their feelings in healthy, nonabusive ways, to understand positive and responsible sexuality, to learn about the legal system, to learn positive thinking and behavioral skills to improve the quality of their relationships, and to reconcile and make restitution to the people who have been affected by their behavior. To accomplish this last goal, victim empathy education is provided along with concrete skills for appropriately managing ongoing sexual urges and temptations. Treatment programs often teach young people to understand the behavioral chains or patterns and cycles of behavior that can lead to sexual misconduct. Children are taught to understand physical, emotional, and social boundaries, and to respect those boundaries in their daily lives.

One of the tools used to encourage and reinforce positive and responsible behavior teaches children about responsible thinking or right thinking, as well as *thinking errors* or wrong thinking. This tool provides children with helpful skills for correcting their own irresponsible thinking patterns that contribute to unhealthy behavior. The children are taught many different types of thinking errors, including ones called *minimizing, justifying, me-me-me* (self-centeredness), and *blaming*. Some of the thinking errors will sound quite familiar, as we all tend to justify or rationalize some indulgence or mistake at some time in our lives, whether it's eating an extra piece of chocolate cake or buying a new computer or widescreen television. Excuse making is something commonly seen in day-to-day life. No evidence exists that proves that minor thinking errors have any negative impact on a child's long-term sexual health.

Most treatment programs seek to help children and adolescents establish core beliefs that are healthy and responsible. These programs challenge and redirect particularly toxic thinking patterns that often reinforce hurtful behavior toward others or that support the idea that a child is inherently a bad person. Good treatment programs work to help children and adolescents develop a healthy *cognitive schema*—a set of attitudes, beliefs, and assumptions that help them interact with their worlds in positive, responsible, sensitive, and wholesome ways.

By learning the different thinking errors that are taught in your child's treatment program, you will learn a valuable skill you can use to help support your child's treatment on a daily basis. As noted earlier, the support and reinforcement a parent can give a child day by day will usually be more influential than anything a counselor can do in an hour or two a week.

Victim empathy education is provided by most treatment programs as a way of helping clients understand the consequences of sexual abuse. Victim empathy education also teaches your child about the effects of his or her actions on others. And realizing the harm he or she has caused helps your child want to build up the barriers that will keep him or her from repeating the hurtful behavior. Some children and adolescents with sexual behavior problems have experienced sexual abuse themselves, as victims, and treatment programs help those clients disclose and discuss their past experiences in order to resolve those experiences in a productive manner.

Relapse prevention programs and *behavior-chain analysis* will teach your child to recognize when an abusive behavior pattern or process is beginning. Such modalities will help teach the youth the needed skills to intervene in such a process before he or she acts out sexually again.

Thinking Errors

The therapeutic community used to believe that before treatment could really begin, a child had to overcome denial. Those same clinicians now understand that denial is common, and that in many cases it can take a long time for children and adolescents to disclose all their inappropriate or hurtful sexual behavior. Almost every child and adolescent with sexual behavior problems struggles with denial or minimization at some point during evaluation and treatment. Denial is simply what a client does to minimize his or her actions, avoid responsibility, excuse the acting-out, and avoid the shame, embarrassment, fear, and other bad feelings associated with getting into trouble for sexual acting-out. Denial is one kind of thinking error. Thinking errors are also called *cognitive distortions* or *wrong thinking*.

Thinking errors are what clients tell themselves in order to minimize, excuse, deny, or rationalize the true extent of a problem, feeling, or behavior. Your child likely used thinking errors to give himself or herself permission to take the next step toward acting out sexually. Thinking errors are one of the major differences between people who act out sexually and those who do not. All people occasionally have inappropriate sexual thoughts, but most people inhibit such thoughts—they prevent themselves from ever acting on them. Children and adults with sexual problems are not successful at inhibiting these thoughts. They use thinking errors to overcome their inhibitions so that they can then act out sexually.

Thinking errors are what we tell ourselves to avoid taking responsibility for the things we do. Taking responsibility means that we admit to the things we've done and the choices we've made, and we agree to accept the consequences for those actions and choices. All of us use thinking errors from time to time, often to avoid criticism or negative consequences. All clients in treatment learn about thinking errors, and they make a personal commitment to do everything possible to avoid using them in their everyday lives. It is very helpful when parents learn about thinking errors, too, so that they can make an effort to confront their children when they are using thinking errors, as well as acknowledge their own thinking errors when the adults notice themselves making those errors, or when their own children point out such errors.

Below is a partial list of thinking errors that are commonly used. This list is only partial. It is possible to come up with many other forms of thinking errors. Labeling thinking errors like the ones listed below helps us pay attention to them and identify them when we use them or hear them.

- *Blaming* occurs when we say or imply that someone else did it or started it or should take responsibility for it. It's also called finger pointing. We use this thinking error to avoid getting into trouble or to avoid embarrassment.
- *Minimizing* occurs when we make something seem less serious than it really is. Some red flags that should alert us when we are minimizing include the words "only" and "just." For example, "I was only five minutes late," or "I just had one cookie." If we convince ourselves that our hurtful or irresponsible behaviors are no big deal, then we won't work on changing them.
- *Justifying* or *Excuse Making* happens when we focus on the "reasons" we didn't do something we were supposed to do or when we did something we weren't supposed to do. Red flags for justifying are words like "but." For example, "I did my treatment work, but my mother picked me up at school so I don't have it." A good way to stop justifying is to stop using the word "but."
- *Me, Me, Me* is when a person thinks only about himself or herself. Me, Me, Me is another way of describing selfishness. In its simplest form, sex offending and sexual behavior problems are possible only for people who think primarily of themselves first. If your child was truly thinking about what would be best for the other person, he or she wouldn't have acted out sexually
- *Victim Stance* happens when we want

people to feel sorry for us or when we are seeking attention. To accomplish that goal, we portray ourselves as the "victim," even when we might have been responsible for doing something wrong. We also use it to get other people to leave us alone instead of holding us accountable when we make mistakes. Sometimes we use this thinking error to get others to do things for us that we should be doing ourselves.

- *Distant Elephants* is the phrase that describes the situation of not thinking ahead about the consequences of our actions. We use this thinking error to avoid the responsibility of controlling our impulses. When an elephant is really far away, it looks small and nonthreatening and is "not a big deal." When the elephant gets close to you, it becomes big, scary, and a "huge deal." To avoid this thinking error, clients are encouraged to always think about the impact of their behaviors ahead of time. Before you act, process the end results of your behavior. Ask yourself, what might happen if I do such-and-such?

- *Denial* happens when we pretend that something isn't true, when it really is. For example, denial happens when we pretend that a friend isn't too affected by alcohol to drive himself home, even though we know he just had four drinks on an empty stomach. Sometimes we refuse to face facts because it makes our lives easier when we ignore what is right before us— but that kind of denial only works for a while.

- *Universals* are global statements that don't leave room for anything else to be true. You may recognize them as "absolutes," "generalizations," "blanket statements," or "black-and-white thinking." Red flags for universals are the words "always" and "never." Any statement that doesn't leave room for anything else is a universal statement.

- *Assuming* occurs when we act as if we know what is going on, but we don't take the time to make sure. We use this thinking error to avoid the responsibility of checking things out with someone else.

- *Lying* is the same as not telling the truth. There are at least three types of lies. One type is leaving information out, holding back, and telling only the parts that make you look good or that the other person may already know about. These are sometimes called *half-truths* or *lies of omission*. When we flat-out say something that is not true, it is a *lie of commission*; we are actively making up a story. The third type of lie is called *a lie of assent*, when we pretend to agree with someone when we really don't. This is also called *faking*. Lying is a common thinking error. Clients are taught that we lie because we don't want consequences. We lie because we don't want to hurt someone's feelings. We lie because we sometimes think that if others think a certain way about us, we will all be happier. These are all lies. We can stop lying so much if we find other ways to get those self-esteem needs met. Clients are encouraged to simply tell the truth, all the time.

- *Avoidance* and *"I Don't Know"* statements take place when we pretend that we don't know the answer that other people need or want. But what is really happening is that we don't want to have to say or think about the truth. A typical adolescent's response to a question about what activity he or she would like to participate in is, "I dunno." We use this thinking error to avoid telling the truth or to avoid sharing information that we are embarrassed about or ashamed of. Most of the time we really do know the answers to questions we are asked, but we don't want to admit it, for fear of the consequences. So, to be responsible, we need to stop using "I don't know" statements.

- *Magical Thinking* or *Super Optimism* is when we believe that everything will work out if we just want it badly enough. We use this thinking error to avoid the responsibility of working to fix our mistakes and taking the necessary steps to make our lives the way we want them to be. For example, a driver who speeds thinks, "I'll never get caught." Or a skier who is reckless thinks, "I'm too good to get hurt." The typical thinking error for people with sexual problems is, "I'll never get acting-out urges again." Magical thinking is wishful thinking, and it usually doesn't work.

- *Diminished-Capacity Syndrome* describes the situations when we pretend that our ability or power was reduced or eliminated because we were upset, stressed, tired, drunk, or "not thinking straight." Examples include, "I was drunk" or "I wasn't thinking; I was too angry." Sometimes young people say things like "I wasn't thinking at the time." Also, sometimes we say, "I forgot" as a way of pretending that we didn't remember something rather than the fact that we made a choice not to think about it at the time. All people are constantly processing thoughts. Clients may not be thinking healthy thoughts, but they are thinking.

- *Acting Helpless* or *Saying "I Can't"* is when we say that we can't do something when the truth is that we simply don't want to. We act helpless or say "I can't" to make it seem like we tried to do something positive but simply were not able to. We claim credit for good intentions, even though we didn't follow through. "I can't" usually really means, "I won't. I'm too embarrassed

or insecure; I don't want other people to laugh at me." It is important that we take charge of our choices and avoid acting helpless.

- *The "I Didn't Have Time" Excuse* is something we use when we pretend to be too busy instead of making active choices or prioritizing our work and activities. This thinking error is one of the most common in a treatment program for young people with sexual behavior problems. Time after time, young people defend their unproductive behavior by saying, "I didn't have time to do it." When their therapist reviews their daily diaries, it becomes clear that they did have time; they simply chose to spend it playing video games or watching television. The responsible thing to say is, "I chose not to do it," or "I chose to do other things instead." Clients are strongly encouraged to take charge of their lives—no excuses, no lies.

Victim Empathy

In treatment, your child will spend a great deal of time learning about how sexual abuse affects victims. Research has shown that sexual abuse may have varying impacts on victims. Some victims have no memory of being sexually abused, while others have recurring dreams, nightmares, anxiety attacks, and flashbacks of the abuse. Both direct and indirect victims of sexual abuse can have many diverse short-term or long-term impacts. Such impacts may also include feeling jumpy, shaky, being easily startled, having trouble concentrating or sleeping, feeling numb, angry, irritable, guilty, or ashamed. Other direct and indirect victims experience feelings of grief and loss, leading to depression, abuse of alcohol or other drugs, problems in sexual relationships, and even suicidal ideation.

If you have experienced sexual abuse and have worked on resolving its effects on your life, this may be a good opportunity to briefly share your experiences with your partner or spouse, your child's counselor, and maybe even your child, to help each of those people understand the personal impact of sexual abuse. Your sharing of your own history may help your child to begin to resolve feelings about his or her own victimization, if he or she, too, suffered abuse. Your child's earlier victimization may have contributed to the child's choice to act out sexually. If your child was not a victim of some type of abuse, this new knowledge about the impact abuse has on victims will help provide an internal barrier to further sexual acting-out, will increase his or her empathy with victims, and will encourage work on victim clarification and restitution.

Your child may react very strongly to the knowledge that someone did to you what he or she has done to another child. Therefore, you should definitely get the advice of a therapist before sharing this information with your child.

As recently as one generation ago, many types of sexual behaviors among children were rarely identified as sexual abuse, and treatment programs were few and far between. That picture began to change as we recognized the terrible toll that secrecy and sexual abuse take on victims and society. It is even possible that you may have engaged in sexual acting-out when you were a child or adolescent. Sometimes, parents end up sharing these experiences with their child when they are angry at the legal system for dealing with their child in what they see as a harsh manner. You are encouraged to discuss such experiences and concerns with your child's therapist in order to get clear, objective feedback about how to best process those feelings.

If you tell your child that you yourself once acted out sexually as a child, it is important that you do so in order to convey that you accept and love your child, no matter what. Do not share such past experiences in order to minimize the seriousness of what your child has done. It is also important that you emphasize that you expect your child to tell the truth, to work hard to accept the consequences of his or her behavior, and to succeed in the treatment program.

Sexual abuse laws have changed a great deal during the past 35 years. Lawmakers are now dealing with sexual abuse in a much more aggressive manner. People working in the field and those impacted by abuse have come to understand that sexual abuse can continue for many years and that cycles of abuse exist, which, if left unchecked, can affect generation after generation of families. We also have learned that we can't afford to ignore the problem. Most states now have things like sex offender registration, sex offender notification, and lifelong civil commitment to help society keep track of sex offenders. While many members of society applaud such efforts to make our communities safer, many others realize that in an effort to hold adult sex offenders more accountable, we are also holding our children and adolescents to adult standards. The consequences youthful sex offenders may encounter are now very severe. As a parent of a child with a sexual behavior problem, you will need to educate yourself about the specific laws and procedures in your state or region in order to best advocate for your child and your family.

We also know that due to the shame, embarrassment, and fear involved in acts of sexual abuse, victims need lots of support to disclose what was done to them, and children and adolescents with sexual behavior problems often need lots of pressure and supportive confrontation to admit to their behaviors, accept treatment, and adopt more responsible lifestyles.

Building Up Barriers

In many treatment programs, your child learns that acting out sexually involves a process that requires overcoming four barriers that normally prevent people from doing such things to others:

1. *Motivation*. Most people don't want to sexually act out. This treatment task involves both finding out where a client's motivation to act out sexually came from, and finding ways to reduce

that negative motivation or those types of sexual feelings or urges.

2. *Internal barriers.* Internal barriers help abusing youth to develop a conscience, learn about how abuse hurts victims, and learn about the laws and the consequences. Some people with sexual behavior problems lack these skills or this knowledge.

3. *External barriers.* These barriers help youth stay out of risky situations, such as babysitting, and avoid unsupervised contacts with vulnerable people.

4. *Victim resistance and sensitivity barriers.* This skill serves as a barrier when a young person thinks about how to protect a potential victim. In addition, a victim's resistance is strengthened when the victim's parents are able to provide good supervision as well as appropriate counseling. Also, clients who are truly sensitive to other people rarely commit sexual offenses.

This process is illustrated in the *Pathways* workbook and in chapter 3 of this book. It is called the *four preconditions model,* and it provides a helpful blueprint for the treatment process. The goal in treatment is to build up all four barriers as high as possible. For people with sexual behavior problems, these four barriers are low, and they can easily be climbed over or pushed through. Your child likely overcame these barriers by using thinking errors to convince himself or herself that acting out sexually was okay, by getting access to victims (often by having poor supervision, babysitting, or playing with younger children), and by using tricks, threats, bribes, or force to get the victim to go along with the sexual behavior. A victim may comply (go along without offering explicit resistance) without giving consent. To help young people build up the "victim resistance and sensitivity" barrier, treatment programs often teach the following rules for true consent.

Rules for Understanding True Consent or Informed Consent

1. True consent requires emotional and intellectual equality.
2. True consent requires honesty.
3. True consent requires equal understanding.
4. True consent requires permission to disagree or refuse without harm.
5. True consent requires equal knowledge about what is going to happen.

To prevent themselves from further sexual behavior problems, clients must learn to build up all four barriers, as shown in the drawing on page 29. For example, your child may begin changing his or her motivation to offend (for example, offenses inspired by strong sexual urges) by speaking more openly about his or her sexual feelings and by learning about new, more appropriate sexual outlets (including the normal teenage activity of masturbation). Clients may also learn some techniques for inhibiting and controlling inappropriate sexual urges. Parents can help their children learn to reduce their motivation to act out sexually by reducing their access to sexually explicit books, magazines, television, and movies and by encouraging physical activity. If you have sexually explicit materials in your home, it is very likely that your child will eventually find and look at such materials. The best option for parents is to simply not have such materials in their homes, garages, vehicles, or outbuildings when they are raising a child or adolescent with a sexual behavior problem.

Understanding Bad Maps and Roadblocks

In some treatment programs for younger children with sexual behavior problems, clients are taught about "bad maps," which are negative or bad life experiences that create trauma in children, or teach children dysfunctional behaviors. Bad maps lead to "roadblocks," which are behaviors or feelings that continue to create problems for children as they get older. Children may be taught that failure to overcome their bad maps may lead them to act out in negative ways, which is sometimes defined as victim behavior. Through this education, children are encouraged to overcome their past negative experiences and become survivors—people who develop healthy, nonhurtful coping skills and behaviors.

Younger children are often trained to identify their dysfunctional life experiences (bad maps) that taught them about inappropriate sexuality. They must then learn healthy ways of identifying and expressing their emotions, as well as understand the significant changes that are happening in their bodies as they approach puberty.

You may find this or other parts of your child's treatment uncomfortable, but it is important that parents participate as much as possible in the treatment process. Current research shows that treatment programs that involve parents fully in the process are more effective than programs that do not. Parents can help their children learn to reduce their motivation to act out sexually by reducing their access to sexually explicit books, magazines, television, and movies, as well as by encouraging physical activity, which generally reduces sexual arousal and sexual drive.

By monitoring and/or changing your child's television and video viewing patterns, you can contribute to your child's treatment. Television viewing can often be a positive, relaxing experience that provides quiet time and helps children settle down or prepare for bedtime. But for children and adolescents with sexual behavior problems, television viewing can also be an addicting activity that keeps them in a passive, inactive mind-set. Television content can be educational or overly stimulating. There is no question that parents of a child with a sexual behavior problem need to carefully consider their child's viewing habits and closely supervise and control his or her access to television and videos. Here are some guidelines to consider:

1. The television should be turned off any time physical, outdoor activities are offered or available. Many children and adolescents with sexual behavior problems are self-indulgent and lethargic. If given a choice, many children—those with and even those without sexual behavior problems—often prefer to sit and watch television. Parents need to actively work to give their children other, healthier choices.

2. Often, it makes good sense to have a rule about keeping the television off during daylight hours. Some families even disconnect their cable during the summer months to encourage sports, other interactive activities, or even reading.

3. Children usually respond well to limits on how much television they can watch. One to two hours per day is plenty. This limit will encourage your child to engage in other, more productive play.

4. Television content should be monitored. In homes where digital cable or satellite TV is available, it is very important to engage the parental controls with a code that your child cannot figure out. Children are creative and inquisitive, and they will watch inappropriate material if they have access to it.

5. Remember that violent content can also be disturbing and harmful to children with sexual behavior problems. Movie and television content ratings should be monitored, and their recommendations followed.

6. Many parents fail to engage parental controls on public access stations or premium channels like Cinemax, HBO, and Showtime. Many such stations show very explicit sexual content. It is probably best to completely block such stations so they are not available at all.

7. Try not to use the television as a babysitter. Get involved with your child, read books, play games, and encourage

physical activities. Because physical activity tends to reduce sexual drive, very sexualized children spend less time engaged in inappropriate sexual behavior when they are involved in physical, large-muscle exercise (such as running, jumping, bicycle riding, rock climbing, swimming, or rowing).

8. Avoid placing a television in a child's bedroom. If children have access to television in their room, they often isolate themselves for hours on end, and they do not interact with others or do healthier physical activities. By taking televisions and video games out of bedrooms, children are much more likely to come out and interact with other family members, which is a positive thing.

Adolescents with sexual behavior problems build up their internal barriers by learning about the impact of sexual abuse on victims and the personal consequences for themselves. For example, after receiving training, your child may use a process called *covert sensitization* as a reminder of the consequences of further sexual acting-out (detention, jail, harm to victims, feelings of humiliation, shame) and to rehearse choosing new, nonoffending behaviors. Younger children learn more basic ways to control sexual feelings, such as exercising or distracting themselves. Your child may also start working on a Healthy Living Project (*Pathways*) or a Safety Plan Book (*Roadmaps*) or some other activity to learn about the impacts of sexual abuse on victims and to help them focus on the positive elements of their lives. When your child begins working on their Healthy Living Project or their victim empathy, you can help by reviewing their work and giving suggestions about other things to add.

Who Is a Victim?

Clients in treatment are taught that many different people are harmed by sexual abuse and sexu-ally inappropriate behavior. In many treatment programs, clients are asked to learn about two different groups of victims: direct victims and indirect victims. Below are some examples of direct and indirect victims.

Direct Victims
- Children who are sexually touched or abused by an older person
- Teenagers or adults who are raped or forcefully molested by another person
- People who see another person exposing his or her private parts to them
- People who receive sexually inappropriate phone calls
- People who have their privacy violated by someone looking through a window at them
- Anyone who is touched sexually and inappropriately in public
- Anyone who is harassed at work or school by another person who makes repeated sexual comments to them

Indirect Victims
- The parents of a child who has been touched or abused by an older person
- The brothers and sisters of any abuse victim
- The husband or wife of a sexual abuse or rape victim
- The boyfriend or girlfriend of a sexual abuse or rape victim
- The parents of a teenager with a sexual behavior problem
- The brothers and sisters of a teenager with sexual behavior problems
- Other relatives of victims or offenders.
- The boyfriend or girlfriend of a teenager with a sexual behavior problem
- Close friends of victims of sexual abuse
- Close friends of the teenager with sexual behavior problems or close friends of the family

The Impact of Sexual Abuse

One of the most important goals of treatment is for clients to learn how their sexual behavior has affected the lives of other people, directly or indirectly. The people listed above as indirect victims may be affected in a variety of ways. For example, the parents of a victim may have to deal with a depressed or anxious child and may have to devote many hours to comforting the child, taking the child to therapy, and spending family resources on doctors' and counselors' bills. In addition, people who are related to or are close to victims may see the world in a negative way. After a loved one has been sexually abused, many people experience ongoing feelings of mistrust, fear, suspicion, or anxiety.

Brothers and sisters of victims or clients with sexual behavior problems often find that their parents spend more time caring for the victim or the client with sexual behavior problems. In some cases, family resources are depleted so that less money and time are available for outings, vacations, family purchases, or even college. Also, some siblings of a client with sexual behavior problems experience verbal abuse or harassment from other kids at school or from neighbors who find out about a sibling's sexual behavior. When each client understands these dynamics, it helps the client to build up necessary internal barriers to help prevent further sexual acting-out.

Supervision, Access, and External Barriers

External barriers are the things that make sexual acting-out impossible, even if the client wants to do it. For example, 24/7 supervision is an external barrier, because children and adolescents can't easily act out if someone responsible is always watching them. In most treatment programs, your child examines all the circumstances surrounding his or her sexual behavior problems and tries to identify the external barriers that might have served as a preventive measure. For example, teenagers with sexual behavior problems frequently act out sexually against younger children while babysitting. An external barrier would be for your

child not to babysit or not to have any unsupervised contact with younger children. Your support for this step is very important.

Here are some supervision guidelines that you should review with your child's treatment provider and follow until the therapist recommends otherwise:

1. Provide constant supervision of your child if any possibility of interaction with younger children exists.
2. Completely stop all babysitting by your child, and help him or her find a way to politely refuse any offers of babysitting jobs (for example, "I'm sorry, I'm not available for babysitting jobs"). Brainstorm with your child about other jobs that he or she could do to replace the money that would have been earned babysitting (such as shoveling walks, mowing lawns, doing errands, washing cars, or walking dogs).
3. Never leave your child alone with any younger children for any reason—not even in an emergency.
4. Do not leave your child alone in the house. Arrange good supervision by a responsible adult who is aware of your child's sexual behavior problems.
5. Make sure your child does not have unsupervised access to community spaces and activities (such as parks, recreation centers, gyms, locker rooms, museums, and camps). Adult supervision should be provided at all times, and those adults should be aware of the child's sexual acting-out history.
6. Allow only adults, not adolescent babysitters, to supervise your child. Children with sexual behavior problems require adult supervision; most teenage babysitters simply don't have the maturity to handle that level of responsibility.
7. Before letting your child go to the home of any friend, make certain that no

younger children are in that home. It is important to talk with the adult in the home about your child's sexual problems and to arrange constant responsible adult supervision.

8. Closely monitor your child's Internet usage and get any computer with Internet access out of the child's bedroom. Children and adolescents with sexual behavior problems require close adult supervision when they are using the Internet. Having Internet access in bedrooms makes this impossible. Such supervision is especially important at the beginning of the treatment process.

You may wonder why such a focus is placed on limiting a client's contact with younger children, especially given that some children and adolescents have had coercive or forceful sexual contact with peers and not with younger children. Other children and adolescents may have exposed their genitals to peers or adults but not committed hands-on sexual abuse. In some cases, a child or adolescent may be in treatment solely because of a preoccupation with sexuality, such as making obscene phone calls, stealing underwear, or compulsively using pornography. You also may wonder why you need to place a restriction on your child's contact with male children when your child may have acted out only with female children.

Research and experience have found considerable overlap in the sexual problems that people develop. It is common for people with one primary sexual behavior problem to get involved in various other forms of sexual behavior as well. For example, research with adults has found that many sexual exhibitionists (those who expose themselves or "flash") have also committed acts of child molestation or rape.

In dealing with children and adolescents with sexual behavior problems, we have found that impulsivity is a common contributing factor to their problems. Impulsivity is about always giving in to urges. When someone is impulsive, he or she thinks or feels something, right away wants to do that thing, and then does it. If given an opportunity, many clients have difficulty resisting their urges to act out sexually, even if they act out in a different way than they have in the past. This range of behaviors is why good treatment programs establish broad rules that help maintain effective external barriers to any form of sexual behavior problem. So a client who has molested female children should also be prevented from being unsupervised around male children. With children and adolescents, research has found that sexual contact with both sexes is common, even for heterosexual individuals. As adults, it is our job to understand the strength of sexual arousal and to help our children make safe decisions by not putting them in situations where they must rely entirely on their own internal barriers.

Your child helps to increase their sensitivity and build up the victim's resistance to future sexual acting-out by going through the victim clarification process and by helping to establish and agreeing to follow new rules at home and in the community, especially when the victim is a family member. During the victim clarification process, your child will be asked to write letters to the victim and to the victim's parents, describing in detail how the sexual acting-out occurred. These letters will be sent only after several drafts are written and polished and only after a thorough discussion is held with your child's counselor. Eventually, your child may get permission to have a meeting in person with the victim and/or the victim's parents to explain that the sexual behavior was not the victim's fault and to establish the rules that the client will need to follow during any and all future contacts (see *Pathways* chapter 11). It is very important to understand that the victim clarification process occurs only if and when the victim is truly ready for such a process.

The second way your child increases their sensitivity and builds up the victim's resistance is by being totally honest and by following all established rules of contact with that victim or with any other vulnerable people he or she may encounter. In addition to limiting and controlling your child's access to potential victims, you can play a crucial role by being on the lookout for certain behavioral clues about your child's potential for further acting-out problems. These clues take two forms: grooming and maintenance behaviors (*Pathways* chapter 6), and the offense behavior chain (*Pathways* chapter 7). These behaviors can be interrupted or redirected by using the relapse prevention plan described in *Pathways* chapter 9 or *Roadmaps* chapter 16 (Safety Plan).

Grooming and Maintenance Behaviors

Grooming behaviors are what your child does to get access to victims and to get them to participate in sexual touching. Grooming can involve several steps: for example, attracting younger kids by playing with certain toys (such as remote-controlled model cars or video games), encouraging a younger child to come for comforting when that child is sad or upset, or setting up a dependent emotional relationship, showing the child pornography, and then gradually increasing the amount of touching involved in the relationship. By understanding grooming behaviors, you and your child will begin to recognize when your child is at higher risk to act out sexually. You can learn to question how much time your child spends at the video arcade, who else is going fishing or camping, where and with whom your child went on a date, or why your child has books and toys that are normally used by younger children.

Maintenance behaviors are the activities and behaviors that your child uses to keep his or her problem sexual behavior going. Reading pornography, thinking or fantasizing about past sexual acting-out, saying hurtful things, acting self-centered, being lazy and avoiding responsibilities, lying, and acting aggressively are all considered maintenance behaviors. Certain high-risk maintenance behaviors are also sometimes called *gateway behaviors*. Gateway behaviors are likely to

lead to further sexual acting-out. Both grooming and maintenance behaviors can be part of your child's acting-out problem, and they are important factors to learn about during a treatment process.

Offense Patterns and Behavior Chains

Some treatment programs are using the concept of offence patterns or cycles to help older clients (age 13 and older) recognize the thoughts, feelings, and behaviors that may lead to inappropriate sexual behavior. Other treatment programs are using something called a *behavior chain analysis* to explore behaviors that may lead to sexual acting-out. Regardless of which approach is being used, it is important that parents learn the concepts and help their adolescents to better understand what led up to their sexual behavior problems.

It is difficult to teach younger children (under age 13) to understand their patterns of behavior or the behavior chains that lead to sexual acting-out. Younger children are often very impulsive, and they have a very hard time understanding what they are thinking or feeling. For such young children, it seems to help if they are taught about things like "danger zones," another name for high-risk situations. Adults also need to recognize that young children think in entirely different ways than adults do. For a young child, a day is a very long, seemingly limitless amount of time, whereas for an adult, a day may feel like a very short time. Children are often focused only on the present and their immediate needs. The ability to anticipate future needs and plan ahead is often developed during early adolescence.

Young children are usually trying to meet some perceived need when they act out. They may or may not know what the need is. The need may be for attention, security, power, or competence. It also may be for anxiety reduction, stress relief, adventure, freedom, or something entirely different. The challenge for adult caregivers is to attempt to figure out what the underlying needs are, then to teach and support more adaptive and healthy ways for the children in their care to meet those needs.

For adolescent clients, the major life events, behaviors, and feelings that your child went through in the months immediately before the sexual behavior problems make up what is sometimes called the *offense behavior chain*. These elements are called *links* in the behavior chain. Before children act out sexually, they have to be in a frame of mind in which they don't care about victims or about themselves. Offenders often report feeling depressed, isolated, bored, or unhappy before acting out sexually. Other clients are simply so impulsive that it doesn't matter what they were feeling before acting out. The intense rush and excitement of sexual behavior can provide a deep (though brief) sense of relief from other life problems.

Some children and adolescents act out sexually for only a short period and have no problem getting their sexual feelings and behaviors under control. Other children and adolescents continue acting out sexually even after receiving consequences and counseling. These children may have a more identifiable behavioral chain that leads to their sexual behavior problems.

Hope for Offense-Free Living: Relapse Prevention and the Development of a Positive Life

Your child can learn to interrupt any offense pattern by using relapse prevention techniques. Regardless of whether your child has an identifiable chain of behaviors that leads to his or her sexual behavior problems, treatment programs will attempt to reduce negative thoughts and behaviors, while building up and encouraging positive thoughts, feelings, and activities.

Your child may learn that early warning signs can signal a possible return to sexual acting-out. Warning signs can include feelings, behaviors, or environmental triggers that put your child in a frame of mind where sexual acting-out would feel good. For example, being rejected by a potential dating partner could trigger some sexual acting-

out against someone who doesn't have the power to say no. Failing a class at school could trigger intense feelings of self-hate. Family conflicts could result in stress and anxiety that could lead to a desire for sexual release. Your child will identify as many warning signs as possible and develop a realistic intervention plan, a way to break up the pattern and get help for each one. By preparing these "safety ropes," "escape ladders," or "escape hatches" to cope with possible temptations and urges to act out sexually, your child will be better prepared to handle life stresses without further sexual acting-out.

Your child may also learn to identify other parts of his or her offense behavior pattern or cycle: seemingly unimportant decisions (SUDs) and high-risk situations (HRSes, pronounced "her-ses"). SUDs are the small decisions and behaviors that can lead to a high-risk situation. HRSes are the situations that clearly increase risk by lowering any of the four barriers (motivation, internal barriers, external barriers, and victim's resistance/sensitivity).

For example, going to a convenience store with two friends who drink beer could be a SUD for an adolescent who has coerced a girl into sex at a party while drinking. If he is invited to one of the friends' houses to drink beer and he goes to the house, it would be a HRS, since it provides an opportunity for poor decision making and for possible sexual acting-out. Relapse prevention and related treatment methodologies not only teach your child to identify these risks on the way toward reoffending, but also help him or her think about ways to avoid these situations or get out of them once they occur.

You are an instrumental part of the process your child will go through in developing a relapse prevention plan. Here are some guidelines for you to keep in mind when you are reviewing your child's plan in a treatment workbook or treatment guide:

1. Observable. Is the warning sign something a parent, counselor, or other

family member can see? Many clients list changes in their feelings (unhappy, depressed) as warning signs, but feelings are not always observable. For example, feeling lonely may be a true warning sign, but you may not necessarily know when your child feels lonely. Therefore, ask your child, "How do you act when you feel lonely?" Those behaviors are then listed as warning signs. When you are reviewing the plan, feel free to ask your child to make changes in it before you sign it.

2. Relevant. Is the warning sign related to sexual acting-out? Ask your child to explain how each warning sign relates to his or her sexual behavior problems.

3. Practical. Is the prevention plan realistic and practical? Many clients list prevention steps such as "Call my counselor." In practice, children rarely, if ever, make the call. Ask your child, "What is a more realistic intervention? Who else would you call so that you can talk about this?"

As a parent, you play a key role in shaping and maintaining your child's relapse prevention plan. The responsibility of using the plan belongs to your child, but you and other key people in your child's life can support the plan by referring to it regularly and reminding your child when you see a warning sign. Ignoring a warning sign takes you a step closer to having your child relapse. When pointing out an observed warning sign, remind your child that you care about him or her and that you are there to help. Consider these remarks from Allen, a 14-year-old who was in transition from a treatment program to self-monitoring.

One of the reasons I have been successful is that my mother reminds me almost every day when I leave the house to keep my barriers up and to avoid children. This reminder helps me remember my treatment, and it also shows me that she cares about me.

Uncovering and Dealing with Past Abuse of Your Child

A final element in understanding how and why your child chose to act out sexually is finding out whether your child has been a victim of sexual abuse and what role that abuse or other experiences might have played in the sexual acting-out. Some (but certainly not all) children and teenagers with sexual behavior problems have been sexually abused themselves, usually during childhood. Terrible as this fact is, it also offers hope by suggesting that sexual acting-out is learned (rather than inherent)—and that what is learned can be changed with new learning. Most adolescents who are sexually abused do not become sex offenders, but there is some relationship between a history of sexual abuse and sexual offending. Recent research suggests that a history of sexual abuse is associated with the likelihood that someone will commit a sexual offense for the first time. Remember, though, many children and adolescents with sexual behavior problems have not been sexually abused. They may have instead learned about sexuality from books, magazines, pornography, movies, friends, or television.[*] Although the previous experience of being sexually abused may be a contributing factor, sexual abuse does not directly cause sexual acting-out. Many (perhaps most) children and adolescents who were sexually abused do not become sex offenders and do not sexually act out. Sexual acting-out is a multifaceted and complex behavioral problem. Treatment will help your child understand that sexual acting-out was the result

---

* Michael C. Seto and Martin K. Lalumiere. "What Is So Special About Male Adolescent Sexual Offending? A Review and Test of Explanations Through Meta-Analysis," *Psychological Bulletin* 136, no. 4 (2010): 526 DOI.

of a series of choices he or she made. Physical, verbal, and emotional abuse, abandonment, and other major life upheavals also may have contributed to your child's choice to act out sexually. By getting help in resolving feelings from past abuse and by learning responsible behavior patterns, your child can learn to make future choices to ensure that no further harmful behavior occurs.

Therapeutic Structures

Individual Therapy: Most programs make individual therapy the cornerstone of treatment. Since sexual behavior is a very private, personal matter, it makes sense that therapy begins with private discussions of sexual issues. Counselors use individual therapy sessions to educate each client about healthy sexuality, to confront thinking errors, to teach relapse prevention techniques or other treatment approaches, and to monitor the client's home, school, and social environment in order to encourage a healthy lifestyle. Many counselors use the CBT, TF-CBT, and DBT approaches described on page 59 and 60. Many counselors start the treatment process with weekly, one-hour counseling sessions. Some parents prefer that their child see only a male or only a female counselor. Most parents have found that the skill and experience of the counselor is more important in providing help for their child than the gender of the counselor. Girls can learn to talk openly with good male or female counselors, and boys can learn to talk openly with good male or female counselors.

Group Therapy: Group therapy for children and adolescents is an effective way to teach clients about relationship skills, impulse control, and constructive ways to express feelings. Group therapy is often a good way to help children and adolescents with poor social skills, low self-esteem, and limited communication skills. Also, when children and adolescents are embarrassed and ashamed about their sexual behavior, they quickly learn in group therapy that they are not alone.

Many parents are concerned that their children might end up learning even worse values from the group or might be exposed to more disturbed or delinquent youths. In a good treatment program, the group leaders exercise strong control over participants and work hard to make sure that positive values, reliable information, and healthy relationships are modeled in the group. Many clients have reported that the only group therapy session they felt awkward about attending was the first one. After meeting other youths with sexual behavior issues, most clients feel supported, and they usually look forward to their weekly sessions. Most outpatient treatment groups meet weekly for 60 or 90 minutes per session. Group therapy is usually less expensive than individual therapy. Many programs use a combination of weekly individual sessions and weekly group sessions throughout the treatment process.

Many parents don't know how to talk with their children about what happens in weekly group therapy. Some parents don't want to embarrass their children, so they ask only very vague or general questions like, "Was group okay today?" Sometimes kids say that their group is confidential, and they can't talk about it. It is important to ask your child's counselor if it is okay to ask questions about what happens in group. In many treatment programs clients are encouraged to talk with their parents about what they learned in group; concerns about confidentiality are easily managed when parents are careful to not redisclose information provided by their child.

Family Therapy: Family therapy is often very important, especially when a child has acted out sexually against someone else living with him or her (siblings, stepchildren, foster children, or vulnerable adults). Involving siblings in therapy ensures that all family members are aware of the treatment rules and healthy boundaries that are taught in treatment. Sexual abuse such as incest is far less likely to occur in homes where open and healthy communication takes place and clear and stable boundaries have been established.

When the victim of a client's sexual behavior lives in the same home, it is important that the victim have his or her own personal therapist to talk to about the abusive behavior. Parents should try to stay involved in their child's therapy by communicating with the counselor regularly and making sure that the counselor is aware of all conflicts and problems in the home, even if the problems don't seem to be related to the client's sexual behavior.

Cognitive-Behavioral Therapies—CBT, TF-CBT, and DBT: CBT refers to cognitive-behavioral therapy, TF-CBT refers to trauma-focused cognitive-behavioral therapy, and DBT refers to dialectical behavior therapy. The term *cognitive-behavioral therapy (CBT)* is a somewhat general term for a classification of therapies with similar features.

There are several approaches to cognitive-behavioral therapy, including rational emotive behavior therapy, rational behavior therapy, rational living therapy, cognitive therapy, and dialectical behavior therapy. Most cognitive-behavioral therapies are based on the idea that our *thoughts* cause our feelings and behaviors, not external things, like people, situations, and events. CBT is based on the scientifically supported assumption that most emotional and behavioral reactions are learned. CBT-based therapies appear to have the greatest empirical support in helping clients overcome a variety of mental health problems, particularly anxiety, depression, and behavioral disorders. The goal of CBT therapies are to help clients *unlearn* their unwanted reactions and to learn a new way of reacting.

Trauma-focused Cognitive Behavioral Therapy: TF-CBT is a structured treatment model that incorporates elements of cognitive-behavioral, attachment, humanistic, empowerment, and family therapy models. It includes several core treatment components designed to be provided in a flexible manner to address the unique needs of each child and family. There appears to be some scientific evidence that this therapy works well in treating trauma symptoms in children, adolescents, and their parents. This model was initially developed to address trauma associated with child sexual abuse and has more recently been adapted for use with children who have experienced a wide array of traumatic experiences.

Here are the specific components of many cognitive behavior therapies:

- Psychoeducation is provided to children and their caregivers about the impact of trauma and common childhood reactions.
- Parenting skills are provided to the parents to optimize children's emotional and behavioral adjustment.
- Relaxation and stress management skills are taught to each child and parent.
- Feeling expression and control skills are taught to help children and parents identify and cope with a range of emotions.
- A client is taught about the relationships among thoughts, feelings, and behaviors. This is called the *cognitive triangle*, and clients are taught how thoughts, feelings, and behaviors all influence one another. Clients and parents modify inaccurate or unhelpful thoughts about the trauma.
- Some types of CBT (TF-CBT) also develop a trauma narrative, in which children describe their personal traumatic experiences.
- Real-life practice of trauma reminders is used to help children overcome their avoidance of situations that are no longer dangerous, but which remind them of their original trauma.
- Joint child-parent sessions help the child and parent talk to each other about the child's trauma.
- The final phase of the treatment is to help clients maintain a safe lifestyle. It teaches adaptive skills that the client may need.

Dialectical behavior therapy: DBT is a system of therapy originally developed by Marsha M. Linehan, a psychology researcher at the University of Washington, to treat persons with borderline personality disorder (BPD). DBT combines standard cognitive-behavioral techniques for emotion regulation and reality testing with concepts of distress tolerance, acceptance, and mindful awareness largely derived from Buddhist meditative practice. DBT has been proven effective in treating some symptoms of mental illness, and it may also be effective in treating clients with mood disorders, sexual abuse survivors, and persons with chemical dependency issues.

Regardless of what specific type of therapy is used with your child, it is important that parents learn as much as possible about the treatment being offered to their child and find out how to support the treatment skills at home in the child's daily life.

Case Management and Case Aide Support: In some areas, agencies may offer in-home counseling, supervision, and case aides who can provide some supervision and home-based support for parents and foster parents. Having a counselor visit your home can be an effective way of building healthy boundaries for children and getting concrete assistance in managing the problems of daily living. Having case aides work with children in the community can be a great way to teach, reinforce, and monitor the skills that are taught in treatment. For example, many counselors work hard to teach clients to avoid interacting with children more than two or three years younger than themselves. Case aides can observe a client's behavior and interactions during community activities and reinforce appropriate behavior while providing valuable feedback to parents and counselors.

Parents As Active Supports in the Treatment Process

Most clients view group therapy as an essential and supportive part of a treatment program. Most clients feel very nervous before their first group session, but then they feel relief and support when they find out that they are not alone in the issues they are facing. In most programs, parents are encouraged to talk with their children about the children's therapy experiences. While therapists in treatment programs will often spend time alone with clients to develop trust and rapport, most therapists want parents to be involved somewhat in the entire treatment process. Many therapists will want to spend part of each individual therapy session talking with parents and getting their feedback. Some therapists also want parents to learn the same material they are teaching those parents' children and teens, so that the parents can support those treatment concepts at home.

By reviewing this *Healthy Families* guide for parents and by participating in their children's counseling whenever possible, parents will become a significant part of the treatment team. Parents are generally encouraged to talk with their children about their child's therapy experiences, respecting the children's rights to privacy, but encouraging them to process aloud with their parents what they are learning and experiencing. By discussing their own individual and group therapy experiences, the children will be able to process what they have learned, making it a more enriching experience.

Parents are advised to ask open-ended questions that encourage sharing. Questions like, "How did group go?" usually are met with answers like, "Fine." Try to ask more probing questions, such as:

- "Who talked the most in group today?"
- "What were the issues discussed in group today?"
- "What did you share in group today?"
- "Who were the leaders in your group?"
- "Who has been in the most trouble in your group lately?"
- "Who in your group is closest to graduation?"
- "How many of your diaries did you do this week?"

- "What are the steps you need to take to make progress in your group?"
- "What treatment work did you go over in group today?"
- "Who do you respect the most in group?"

The following questions may help a parent monitor his or her child's individual treatment progress:

- "What treatment assignments do you have this week?"
- "How have you done on your daily diaries?"

- "What do you need to do to get your treatment work done this week?"
- "How are you doing at catching yourself using thinking errors?"
- "What are your biggest temptations for looking at pornography?"
- "How honest are you able to be with your counselor?"
- "What have you learned in counseling this week?"
- "What is the hardest thing about your counseling so far?"

Chapter 6

Siblings: Silent Sufferers

Parents of children with sexual behavior problems often find they are spending much more time than usual with the child who has acted out sexually. Supervision needs to increase, and parents often spend hours each week taking the child to meetings with social workers or lawyers and to assessment or treatment appointments. When one child has committed sexual abuse against one or more children in the home, the time and energy demands are frequently even more extreme, since parents try to juggle normal work and household tasks with additional meetings and appointments for the victim as well as the abuser. In addition, the supervision needs are intense. Parents faced with sexual abuse in their home often have to rethink every event of daily living in order to maintain effective supervision. Sometimes, parents have to find another living arrangement for the child with the sexual behavior problem, and that can involve parents splitting up for a period of time or having to rent another home or apartment. These developments often have serious emotional and financial impacts on entire family systems, and the siblings of the abuser often find their lives have changed in significant and unpleasant or uncomfortable ways.

In families with several children, an uninvolved sibling (a brother or sister other than the abuser or the victim) is frequently overlooked. Many well-meaning parents try to protect the abuser's privacy or their other children's innocence by not telling the other children about what has happened. In some families, the uninvolved siblings have already found out part or all of what happened, either from the victim or by observing family dynamics. For example, it is hard not to know that something serious has happened when police officers are coming into your home. Parents often struggle with decisions about which family members should be told about their child's sexual behavior problem. In the case of siblings, here are some general guidelines to consider:

Very young children (under six years of age) may be too young to understand what happened. In such cases a parent should provide very basic information, such as that their older brother or sister did some "wrong touching" and now is going to see a counselor and may be living elsewhere for a while. With older children, it is often a good idea to explain about the court process, or explain more detail about laws that make sexual touching illegal in some cases. Parents are often surprised that their older children have already figured out what has happened in their family. Many parents want to protect their children from having to know about sexual touching and illegal behavior, only to find out later that their child has listened into conversations or read papers that have been left out. Of course, every parent must make their own decision about what to share with their children, based on the unique circumstances in their family, including the maturity of the children.

Other younger siblings may have been abused or exposed to sexual behavior, as well. Parents need to get professional help in talking with all their children to discover whether those children were involved in or witnessed the known sexual abuse. Keep in mind that many younger siblings may be afraid of getting into trouble or disrupting the family. It is very common for younger siblings to deny having had sexual experiences with older siblings, only to have the abuser later admit during therapy that other siblings were involved. Just because a younger sibling says that nothing happened does not necessarily mean that that child's statement is true.

Older siblings, such as teenagers, can usually figure out what has happened, and it is often best to tell them about it rather than trying to maintain a family secret. It is important that older siblings understand that a great deal of family attention will need to be devoted to dealing with the sexual abuse issues. It is also important to get the older siblings' support in changing family rules and boundaries so that no further sexual abuse occurs.

Remember that having accurate information is sometimes very reassuring for children. By explaining the situation to them, the children often feel more involved and secure with what is happening. When the family is in crisis but nobody is talking about it, it can be very stressful and confusing to a young child.

Consider this account written by Angie, an 18-year-old whose teenage brother was charged with molesting some neighbor children:

It was February of my senior year of high school when my younger brother, Benny, was accused of sexually molesting the three children who lived across the street from us.

It was a typical day, or so it seemed. I came home from school one afternoon and nobody was home. Usually, Benny was already home from school before me, but that day he wasn't. After some searching for a possible note that would tell me where he was, I called my dad. I got no answer, so all I could do was wait until one of them called. Finally, about an hour later, my dad and Benny walked in the door. I asked where they had been, and my dad's response to my question was, "At the police station." I couldn't tell whether this was a joke or not, but by the look on my dad's face, I was guessing it wasn't.

"What happened?" I asked. That's when the story unfolded. The children across the street had accused Benny of sexually

molesting them. I was bewildered by what was being told to me, but I kept listening. The officer investigating the accusation wanted Benny to come in for questioning. My dad said that he asked Benny some questions; all the while, Benny was maintaining his innocence.

Months passed and no word came of the investigation. It seemed like this whole incident had disappeared, until one day when a letter came in the mail from the juvenile court. It stated that Benny was being charged with two counts of child molestation and that he was to appear in court for a fact-finding hearing. Along with the summons was more information about who would be representing Benny and what to expect of the court process. My dad called the lawyer who would be representing Benny and asked what his options were. The lawyer told him that Benny could plead not guilty or innocent, but if he pleaded innocent and was found guilty, the penalty would be heavier.

My dad told me that he had a feeling Benny wasn't telling the whole truth, and he called the lawyer to see what he could do to find out the truth. The lawyer advised that Benny should take a polygraph test, and, if he passed it, we could use that in his favor. The day came when Benny was to take the polygraph, and he was swearing his innocence until the end. When I came home from school he wasn't home yet, but I assumed he was on the way home. The phone rang, and it was my dad. He was silent for a while and then he said, "He failed it." I didn't know what to think. I was stunned. My dad told me not to talk to Benny about it and said that we would discuss it when he got home. Benny came home minutes later and walked in like nothing was wrong.

Benny was playing on the computer when my dad came home. As soon as he walked in, my dad told Benny to get off the computer. I don't know what my dad was feeling, but from the looks of it he was so shocked he was angry. The three of us sat and talked about the polygraph, and Benny kept saying, "I don't know." I was supposed to go to work later that afternoon, but I was so upset and traumatized by the situation that I didn't go.

August 16 came, the day before Benny was supposed to be in court. We all went out to dinner that night. I don't remember what we had been talking about, but Benny made the comment that this would probably be the last dinner he would have with us. I think he knew he would be put into the detention center.

August 17—the day I will never forget. After passing through the metal detector, I saw all the kids waiting. I couldn't believe how many kids were in trouble for something or other. I looked at them and then I looked at my brother. I thought to myself that Benny didn't look like the type of kid to be in trouble. We waited for about two hours, and then Benny was called into the courtroom. We walked into the room, where his attorney, the probation officer, and the prosecutor joined us. The hearing took place, and the final decision was that Benny was found guilty of child molestation. He was sentenced to 30 days in detention, and he was also put on probation for two years.

This was the hardest day for me. I remember seeing a man come out the side door to take Benny away. The man put Benny into handcuffs and started walking him to the door. As Benny reached the door, I was sitting in the seat closest to the door, and he reached out to me, crying. My dad and I walked out of the courtroom. I was crying uncontrollably. We went down to the detention center. We waited until Benny was processed into the system. Then my dad was allowed to see him while I sat wait-

ing (siblings were not allowed to visit). The only time I would be able to talk with Benny in the coming month would be during his occasional phone calls home.

Benny had a review hearing a few days later, and it was there that he was ordered to move out of our neighborhood for his entire two years of probation. Finally the day came when Benny was released from detention. He and my dad rented an apartment nearby, but out of the neighborhood. My dad asked if I would live by myself in the house, to take care of it. After several months of loneliness, I found myself getting strange looks and stares from my neighbors. Families that I used to babysit for would now look the other way and ignore me. Children I used to see and talk to in the neighborhood would run inside when I was outside.

Angie's brother's behavior clearly had a severe impact on her. Her life changed significantly, and she became a very important part of Benny's treatment team. Angie was approved as a chaperone for Benny, because she demonstrated the maturity and responsibility to take on such a role. This was unusual since she was only 18 years old. She often drove Benny to his counseling appointments, and she sometimes participated in some of the counseling sessions so she could talk about what she was experiencing and learn how she could support Benny's treatment. Without Angie's understanding and support, Benny would have experienced far more difficulty in treatment. Angie sometimes helped supervise Benny, and she also helped motivate him to complete his treatment work. Since Benny and Angie lived alone with their father, Angie took on more of a parental role than is common with older siblings. In Benny's case, her involvement was very helpful.

Nonvictim siblings are considered to be indirect victims of a client's sexual behavior problems because family dynamics usually change considerably after a client's sexual behavior is discovered. Family finances are often stressed, parental conflict may increase, and all family members may feel the shame and stigma of being associated with a child or adolescent who has a sexual behavior problem. The following suggestions may be of assistance in preventing siblings from being negatively affected by a client's sexual behavior problem:

- Talk with all children about how the client's problems have affected them.
- Take some private time with each sibling every week and make sure that his or her needs are being met.
- Consider involving all the siblings in some counseling sessions to help them talk about their reactions to the client's behavior.
- Avoid secrets in the family. If the siblings are old enough to understand what is happening, talk to them about what is going on. The uncertainty and anxiety of not knowing are usually harder to handle than the truth. Some parents choose not to tell younger siblings about an older sibling's sexual behavior problems in order to protect the younger children's innocence or to protect the privacy of the older sibling. While this choice may be appropriate with very young children, children in elementary school and older often realize that something important is going on in the family, and their anxiety is often reduced when parents tell them the truth about the trouble their older sibling is in. As stated above, younger children often don't need to know all the details, but telling them that their sibling is in trouble for doing "inappropriate touching" is often a good compromise.

- Try to buffer the impact on siblings. For example, a client may be prohibited from being around children, so a younger sibling might not be allowed to have a friend spend the night. Try to make sure that siblings can still have normal relationships with their friends. This approach sometimes requires creativity and flexibility. For example, one client spent one weekend each month with his grandparents so that his younger siblings could have friends spend the night.
- Be aware that most good treatment programs require that the client be the one to follow the treatment rules. This particular requirement, however, can set up an unhealthy power dynamic. For example, each client will most likely be given a rule that says being alone in a room with younger siblings is totally off limits. Some younger siblings are very understanding and avoid rooms where a client is playing, but other siblings may develop a sense of power over the client and intentionally "wander" into rooms where the client is, making it necessary for the client to leave the room. Parents need to be aware of these possible dynamics and talk with all the children about such situations. Sometimes it makes sense to give some rules to younger siblings, too, to help everyone work together to maintain a safe home.

Chapter 7

Helping the Victim, Creating a Healthy Environment, and Protecting Your Children from Further Abuse

As a parent, your main focus is probably on protecting your child from acting out sexually again. If the victim is another of your children in the same home, you are undoubtedly torn between caring for one child and wanting to protect the other. Even if the victim is not a family member, it is essential that some care and attention go to the victim. You may be able to encourage the victim's parent or parents, in an open, caring, nonblaming way, to seek professional counseling for the victim. A counselor trained in working with victims of sexual abuse can help the victim understand what happened so that he or she can develop coping skills for recovering from the abuse and minimizing future emotional harm or scars.

Parents of children with sexual behavior problems need to think about one additional concern: children and adolescents with sexual behavior problems may be more susceptible to future sexual abuse by others. This fact may be due to the youth's impulsivity, precocious interest in sexuality, or other factors.

In this chapter you will learn how to identify boundary invasions, which is when some other person violates a personal or professional boundary and tries to establish an inappropriate relationship with your child. Years of experience with sexual offenders has taught professionals that sexual grooming often precedes sexual abuse of children and adolescents. We have also found that sexual grooming usually involves boundary invasions, and by intervening and stopping boundary invasions, it is possible to stop sexual grooming before any sexual abuse occurs.

If you are the parent of both the abuser and the victim, it is usually best to seek different counselors for those two children. The abusing child's counselor may want to meet with the victim periodically, especially if the family is working toward ongoing contact and reunification. The main reason for having two counselors is that one counselor simply can't represent the best interests of both the abusing child and the victim. The victim deserves to have someone looking out only for his or her interests.

Consider the following comments from the mother of an adolescent who molested his younger sister in the parent's home:

> It is apparent to me how easily the victims seem to get put on the back burner, because you are immediately fighting for the rights of your offending child. Being a mother of both the victim and the offender, I listen to other parents talk about the victim's family, not necessarily in a negative way but it is obvious they don't really understand what the victim goes through, having to process and reprocess, live with the abuser, changes in family activities, and new restrictions and rules. It is clear to me that it is incredibly hard work to effectively meet the needs of both the abuser and the victim in the same home!

Your understanding of the effects of sexual abuse and your support for the clarification and restitution process can go a long way toward helping your child understand the harm he or she has caused and allowing your child the opportunity to attempt to undo a degree of the damage caused.

In some treatment programs, restitution is defined as more than just paying for the victim's counseling. Restitution means making things better, and trying to do everything possible to repair the damage that was done by the abusive behavior.

In the clarification process, clients make clear to themselves and their victims exactly what happened during the sexual incidents so that clients can accept full responsibility and victims can escape the corrosive effects of self-blame. During the early stages of clarification, your child will learn about victim-impact issues; in later stages, your child will write a series of letters to the victim and the victim's parents (including to you, if the victim is in your own family). The letters may or may not be sent, depending on circumstances such as the client's relationship to the victim, the restriction of court orders, and the wishes of the victim and the victim's family. In these letters, your child will clarify who was responsible for the abuse, address the feelings of the victim in a concrete and meaningful way, explain exactly what happened, and try to restore to the victim the sense that although something valuable was stolen, the victim is not "contaminated" and does not need to feel ashamed.

This clarification process also gives the victim an opportunity to share his or her thoughts or feelings and ask any questions they may have. The clarification process is designed to be victim centered for the purpose of aiding the victim's healing. During the treatment process, clients sometimes have to be reminded that "it is not about you, it is about making things better for the victim."

As a parent, you may worry that by writing these letters your child will be "reopening the victim's wounds." Experience with victims has shown that clarification letters and meetings can go a long way toward helping victims overcome feelings of shame and fear related to the abuse. The victim also needs to hear directly from the client that the abuse experience was different from the special sexual sharing that she or he and a chosen partner will have later in adulthood.

If the victim is a family member, you should review the clarification letter to make sure it is appropriate. Appropriate in this case means that the letter contains no thinking errors and does not overtly or subtly blame the victim, ask for sympathy, or make light of the abuse. The letter is always given to the victim's parents first—and, if the victim is in counseling, to his or her counselor. Both parents and counselor then determine whether the letter is appropriate for the victim to receive.

Sometimes a client is asked to write a clarification letter to the parents of the victim and even to his or her own parents, in order to apologize for everything he or she has done to harm both families. If the victim was very young (under six years old), the client may be asked to compose a future letter that is written in adult language so that when the victim grows up, an adult apology letter will be waiting, in case the victim wants to know more about his or her childhood abuse. Such future letters are usually given to the parents of the victim for safekeeping.

If you are the parent of both a client and a victim, you may find yourself torn between wanting to protect your child-victim and wanting to support your child who has the problem sexual behavior. Remember, the most important thing you can do is to maintain strong external barriers (good supervision) so that opportunities to act out sexually are minimized. Protecting your child-victim also supports your child-client's treatment. Since being the parent to both youths is extremely difficult for a parent, you may want to find a counselor of your own so you can openly talk about your confusion, discomfort, pain, and fear.

In the final part of the clarification process, a series of meetings may be held. The meetings should be supervised by the victim's counselor, in cooperation with the counselor for your child with the problem sexual behavior. Both the abuser and the victim may experience a great deal of anxiety before these meetings. During the meetings, it is the abuser's job to explain to the victim, the victim's parents, and the victim's counselor exactly what happened, to accept full responsibility, and to acknowledge at least some of the harm done to the victim and his or her family. The purpose of the meeting is to make things better for the victim, so the actual structure of the meeting will depend on the victim's wishes and the victim's counselor. It may take several meetings to allow the victim enough time and opportunity to clarify his or her feelings about the client. Permission for victims and clients to have even supervised contact should not be given until after these meetings occur and should depend on their successful outcome. For parents who want to get their family back together, this can be a frustrating wait, but it is very important to the victim's sense of safety.

The clarification process is the primary way clients begin to make restitution for their actions. Restitution is not revenge, but rather a way to begin to balance the harm done. Just as your child can never forget that he or she has acted out sexually, your child can remember that he or she has done everything possible to make amends to the victim or victims. By participating in the clarification process, your child also learns on a much deeper level how much harm sexual abuse does to victims. This knowledge helps your child build up his or her internal barriers to reoffending, as well as helps the victim build up resistance to ever being abused again.

Consider the thoughts of one couple who have been supporting their child in a sexual behavior treatment program for about one year:

> Helping our child during treatment has included strengthening our "external barriers" by replacing our child's cell phone with one that has only preprogrammed numbers, and no picture or text-messaging capability. We also have installed parental control software on all of the home computers and alarms on the bedroom doors and windows of all our children.

As parents of a child with a sexual behavior problem, you can practice some critical parenting skills that will help create a healthy living environment for your child. Some important core parenting skills are listed below:

- *Encourage constructive communication with your child.* Take time each day to talk to each of your children about their experiences and feelings that day.
- *Encourage appropriate affection.* Hugs, side hugs, and pats on the back are very important reinforcement for children and adolescents.
- *Give praise for responsible and positive behavior.* Show your children that you are proud of them for all the things they do right. Such praise will help counter the very negative self-esteem impacts that sexual behavior problems can cause.
- *Eat meals together at least once a day.* Turn off the television and interact during these meals. Mealtimes are important opportunities to teach social skills, support positive behavior, and learn about your children's activities.
- *Avoid activities that may increase sexual thoughts or sexual feelings.* Those activities can include jokes or innuendoes about sex, swear words, or pornographic magazines and movies. Even if you think such materials are hidden out of sight, children and adolescents will find them. Get them out of the house.
- *Move televisions out of bedrooms.* Televisions in bedrooms encourage social isolation, distract children from reading and doing school activities, and provide opportunities for children to view inappropriate material. Even soap operas and talk shows can expose children to concepts for which they are not yet ready.
- *Abide by the parent rating systems for movies, television, and music.* You can avoid overstimulating your child by closely following the movie, television, and music rating guides. For example, if a video is

rated PG-13, wait until your child is 13 before allowing him or her to view it.

- *Take time to have fun with your child.* Your child should know that you enjoy spending time with him or her.

- *Tell your children you love them.* This suggestion applies to both mothers and fathers. Try not to let a day go by that you don't tell your children you love them. This goes for your spouse, also. Your children benefit from hearing you say loving things to your spouse.

- *Help your children choose appropriate clothing.* Some children want to look "sexy" or older than they really are, but children and adolescents should dress in an age-appropriate manner. Parents should make sure that their children's clothing is not too revealing and that it is neat and clean. The state of a child's clothing can reveal his or her self-esteem.

- *Pay attention to hygiene.* You would be surprised how many children are not expected to brush their teeth at least once or twice daily. Some children are allowed to wear dirty clothes and are not required to shower regularly. Though the children are often coping as best they can, they do not have the resources or the knowledge to offset such neglect. Pay attention to the details: establish a routine in your home where children always brush their teeth before going to bed, take regular showers or baths with soap, and wear clean clothes.

- *Maintain bathroom privacy rules.* Make sure that your child does not use the bathroom at the same time as other children. Also make sure that your children learn to shut the bathroom door when they are in it. Likewise, they need to learn to knock on doors before entering them.

- *Pay attention to the ages of your child's playmates.* Generally, it is a good idea to make sure that children play with other children who are within two or three years of their age. Any and all play with much younger children should be closely supervised by adults.

- *Watch out for the onset of puberty.* With puberty comes an increase in sexual feelings and behavior. Many, many parents are caught off-guard when their children start demonstrating sexual behaviors during puberty that they had not demonstrated when they were younger.

- *Be discreet about parental sexual behavior.* It is positive for children to see welcome-home hugs or brief kisses between parents, but too much touching and hugging in front of children can stimulate their own sexual feelings.

- *Control your own inappropriate verbal and aggressive behaviors.* Find ways to deal with anger other than yelling, swearing, hitting, shoving, throwing or breaking things, slamming doors, and screeching tires. Often children with sexual behavior problems were traumatized as very young children by witnessing violence or sexual abuse.

- *Maintain an identifiable schedule and structure within your home.* Regular bedtimes, mealtimes, hygiene times, and chores all help a child to develop positive and healthy routines and habits. Such structures give a child something to fall back on when he or she is old enough to live alone. Lack of structure can lead to boredom and to a search for excitement that results in sexual acting-out. It is the parents' job to establish and reinforce such clear and reliable routines.

- *Eliminate pornography in your home.* Some parents use mainstream, adult-oriented pornography in the privacy of their own bedroom. Years of experience with children and adolescents has proven, time and time again, that such pornography gets discovered and used by children. If you have such materials, it would be best to get those items out of your home. Remember the adage, "The apple doesn't fall far from the tree." If you can't manage your own addictive behaviors, such as pornography use, don't expect your child to be able to manage it either.

- *Maintain good control over media and Internet usage in your home.* If you have computers that access the Internet, locate them in main living areas that allow for good visual supervision. Avoid letting children have computers or televisions in their bedrooms. If your children use the Internet, make sure that appropriate screening software is installed on their computers, and make sure that you check the history on the Internet browser very often.

- *Be aware of how media access to sexual content can trigger and reinforce sexual behavior problems and urges.* Make a point to monitor your child's CDs, iPod music libraries, and MP3 players. Also, be aware that many portable electronic devices have built-in wireless Internet access, such as the Sony PSP, the Nintendo DSI, and the iPod Touch. Most laptop computers now have wireless Internet, and even though you may not have wireless capability in your home, kids may be able to stand by a window and access the Internet from a neighbor's wireless connection. Many phones also have Internet access. It is very common and easy for kids to download pornography onto their smartphone.

- *Monitor and pay attention to your child's online profile, e-mail addresses, and social networking activities.* MySpace and Facebook are social networking sites. If your child has an account on one of those sites, visit it regularly and check the profile. Communicate regularly with your child about how he or she responds to inappropriate or weird e-mails, comments, etc.

- *Take an interest in your child's schoolwork and treatment program and homework.* Develop a time and a routine for helping your child get such responsibilities done. Review your child's schoolwork often, and go online to your child's school to check on his or her progress. Always attend parent-teacher meetings or treatment team meetings in your child's residential facility. Sometimes it is possible to attend by phone if you live a long way from the facility.

- *Support positive physical activities.* Go for walks with your children and support their involvement in organized sports. Remember, physical activity can help compete with sexual arousal. Physically active children will be better equipped to manage their sexual feelings.

- *Watch for boundary invasions and take steps to make sure that your child is not being groomed for sexual contact by other adults.*

Understanding Boundaries and Watching Out for Boundary Invasions

In addition to the personal problems with which they are dealing, children and adolescents with sexual behavior problems sometimes are also themselves more vulnerable to sexual abuse by older adolescents or adults. The added vulnerability may be because these youth are more sexualized and demonstrate more precocious sexual behaviors than their peers, or it may be due to other factors such as impulsivity, emotional neediness, or poor supervision.

Parents and caregivers can play key roles in preventing such future abuse by increasing their awareness of sexual grooming processes to which their children may be exposed and by learning specific things to watch for when caring for their children. The concluding pages of this chapter are designed to help parents become more vigilant supervisors in order to allow them to identify and stop potential abusers from having access to their children.

As a parent, you have probably heard about situations where a trusted member of the public, such as a teacher, mentor, or coach, has been accused or convicted of a sexual offense. Web sites such as www.badbadteacher.com provide details of the many hundreds of such cases that have occurred in the United States over the past few years. A report ordered by Congress and released in 2004 examined previous studies and surveys of teacher sexual misconduct and sent a troubling message. It estimated that 9.6 percent or some 4.5 million students out of 50 million in American public schools "are subject to sexual misconduct by an employee of a school some time between kindergarten and 12th grade."[*]

You might ask yourself, "How can this happen?" To understand that, it is helpful to know a little about the sexual grooming process. Sexual grooming almost always precedes sexual molestation of vulnerable people. Sexual grooming is accomplished by boundary invasion. It is our goal to prevent sexual grooming by preventing inappropriate boundary invasion behaviors.

Sexual grooming is sometimes difficult to spot. Here is a summary of what often happens in sexual grooming:[†]

1. The potential abuser identifies a vulnerable person.
2. The potential abuser engages the victim in peerlike involvement.
3. The potential abuser desensitizes the victim to touch.
4. The potential abuser isolates the victim.
5. The potential abuser works to make the victim feel responsible.

According to the 2004 U.S. Department of Education report referenced earlier, school district staff are not being trained in how to recognize or prevent educator sexual misconduct. The report related that any employee, including volunteers, might molest a student. It also found that educator sexual offenders are often well-liked and considered to be excellent teachers. Special education students or other vulnerable students are often targets of sexual offenders. The DOE report said that adults who have access to students before or after school or in private situations (coaches, music teachers, etc.) are more likely to abuse than those who don't.

The blurring of professional relationships is also called a *boundary violation* or *boundary invasion*, and it occurs when a professional person goes beyond what is associated with his or her professional role and establishes another type of relationship with someone or with that person's family. Here is a list of possible boundary invasions that often precede sexual grooming. These are behaviors that should raise red flags with parents. By knowing these boundary invasions, you will be better able to protect your children from potential sexual abuse:

- Taking an undue interest in a child (i.e., having that child become a "special" friend or establishing a "special relationship" with that child).
- Giving gifts or money to a young person for no legitimate, approved reason.
- Engaging in peerlike behavior with a young person (i.e., being "cool" by behaving or talking like a teenager).
- Being overly "touchy" with certain children or teens.
- Favoring certain young people by giving them special privileges.
- Talking to a child about problems that

---

[*] Shakeshaft, Charol. *Educator Sexual Misconduct: A synthesis of existing literature.* 2004 U.S. Dept. of Education. Available at www2.ed.gov/rschstat/research/pubs/misconductreview/report.pdf.

[†] Adapted from Carla Van Dam, *Identifying Child Molesters: Preventing Child Sexual Abuse by Recognizing the Patterns of the Offenders* (New York: The Haworth Press, 2001).

would normally only be discussed with peers (e.g., the adult's marital problems).

- Talking to a child or adolescent about the youth's personal problems to the extent that the professional becomes a confidant of the youth when it is not the professional's job to do so.
- Allowing the young person to get away with inappropriate behavior—an example of "playing favorites."
- Being alone with the child or teen behind a closed door in a facility.
- Giving the young person rides in the adult's personal vehicle for other than approved trips.
- Initiating or extending contact with a young person beyond the workday.
- Using e-mail, text messaging, or instant messaging to discuss personal topics or interests with the child or adolescent.
- Invading a young person's privacy (e.g., walking in on the youth in the bathroom).

- Taking the young person on personal outings outside of work hours.
- Telling sexual jokes to the child or teen.
- Engaging in talk containing sexual innuendo or banter with the youth.
- Talking about sexual topics that are not related to a specific curriculum.
- Showing pornography to a youth.
- Hugging, kissing, or other physical contact.

Many children benefit greatly from healthy, respectful relationships with adult mentors, friends, neighbors, and family members, and most such relationships do not result in sexual abuse. By being aware of the red flag behaviors listed above, parents will be better able to make sure that their child is involved in healthy, non-abusive, non-grooming relationships. Remember, if we stop inappropriate boundary invasions, we've stopped sexual grooming, which means we have stopped sexual abuse!

Chapter 8

Family Reunification: Putting the Family Back Together and Developing a Healthy Environment

If your child has abused a brother or sister, it is normal for the child or adolescent with the sexual behavior problem to be placed outside the home for a period of time so that he or she can complete the assessment process and begin treatment in a safe place where reoffending will be less likely. Sometimes children and adolescents are sent to stay with other family members or church members, or they may go to foster homes, friends' homes, or residential treatment facilities. When a client's behavior is very aggressive or he or she has other serious conduct problems, the client may need to be placed in a juvenile correctional institution or a residential treatment facility.

Regardless of where the client has been living since the abuse was discovered, the return home can be a complicated and important process, and is one that requires careful planning. A primary goal of the reunification process is to ensure that no further victimization occurs by reducing risk possibilities within the home.

Sometimes parents expect that their child's treatment will be completed while the child is away. *Please remember that your child's treatment is really just beginning when he or she returns home.* When a client returns to the home where a victim or another vulnerable person resides, he or she must put into practice all the skills learned during treatment. Returning home means that the client will encounter people and situations that may trigger arousing or disturbing memories and feelings. Returning a client to a home where victims or other vulnerable people reside can sometimes result in reoffenses.

The most important goal of the reunification process is to reduce the risk to previous victims or other vulnerable people, including nonabused brothers and sisters, frail or elderly adults, or anyone living in the home who is physically or developmentally disabled or challenged.

One of the biggest mistakes a parent can make in this situation is to allow the client to be alone with a victim or vulnerable family member in an attempt to let the client build trust and "prove" that the treatment he or she received has worked. Unfortunately, this mistake has resulted in far too many reoffenses. Children and adolescents with sexual behavior problems should be expected to show that they have made treatment progress by doing everything possible to avoid being alone with victims or other vulnerable people, and by avoiding other high-risk situations. They can show their treatment commitment by following all agreed-upon house rules and by making an active effort to seek out supervision rather than trying to avoid or get around supervision by adults.

The reunification process should be guided by the following overall assumptions:

- Victim readiness is the most important factor and reunification should not occur until the victim's treatment goals are met. This includes trauma integration and symptom reduction.
- The reunification process must be designed and agreed upon by the victim's therapist and the abuser's therapist working together.
- The victim and victim's well-being is at the center of this process.

- Abusive and dysfunctional family dynamics need to be resolved prior to beginning the reunification process.

Please consider the following example of a reunification process for a 13-year-old adolescent who had sexually abused his younger sister:

> I became an abusive person because I watched my dad during my childhood. All those years he was very disrespectful to my mother, and it felt like he respected me more than he respected my mother. I was never directly abused by anybody, but I watched as my dad yelled at my mom, cussed at her, and told her that she was wrong. Sometimes he would just walk away angry, and I wouldn't understand what had happened. I tended to take his side, and I blamed my mom. In those years, I also looked at a lot of pornography. It, too, was abusive of and violent toward women.
>
> What I have learned is that I want to break this pattern of abuse. I remember that during my evaluation I told my mother that I hated her. After a few months of treatment I came to realize how abusive I had become. I confronted my father, who agreed with me and promised to go to counseling himself to change his behavior. I am also working to change my own abusive behavior, and I have even told my mother that I truly love her. I can see now how it became easy for me to sexually abuse my sister. I believed I was in charge, just like my dad, and I believed that I could do whatever I wanted and nobody could stop me. One time I was so violent my parents had to call the police. Now, I am committed to doing treatment, and to breaking this pattern of abuse.

This example clearly illustrates how sexual behavior problems can develop as a result of complex family dynamics. It also illustrates how focusing all treatment on the abusing child or adolescent will sometimes miss other treatment targets. In this case, if the boy's father was unwilling to seek help on his own, the underlying patterns of abusive and disrespectful behavior may not have been resolved, and after the adolescent returned home he would be at increased risk of returning to abusive behavior. It is very important for parents of children and adolescents with sexual behavior problems to look critically at their own patterns of behavior and be willing to explore and resolve those issues as part of their child's treatment process.

On the next two pages you'll find a summary of how a safe, gradual reunification process might work with a client who is returning to a home where a victim or a vulnerable person resides.

Parents often ask what kinds of safeguards should be set up to protect against a reoffense when their child is reunited with a victim or when the child moves back into a home where younger children live. Part of the victim clarification process is set up so that the abuser, the victim, and the parents can agree on visitation and reunification rules that provide new, stronger boundaries and barriers to offending behavior within the home. All family members should sign the rules document after it is developed by the client's therapist, and changes should be made only with the permission of that therapist.

General Reunification Protocol for Children or Adolescent Sexual Abusers Who Are Returning to Homes Where Vulnerable Children or Adults Reside

Note: These are general guidelines only. The actual reunification process for your child may differ from that presented here, depending on the severity of his or her sexual acting-out, the effectiveness of supervision within the home, and other related factors. Progress from one step to the next always depends on the child's progress in treatment and the parents' understanding of the need for supervision.

1. The youth completes a thorough assessment by a treatment provider experienced in child and adolescent sexual problems. *Note:* This is best done soon after the youth's abusive behavior is discovered.

2. The victim in the family is assessed and counseled by a specialized victim therapist. Other children in the family are also seen by the victim's therapist and/or the abuser's therapist to talk about his or her experiences with the abuser and how vulnerable the victim or other siblings might be to any future sexual abuse.

3. The youth starts treatment and completes a thorough sexual history. The young person meets with his or her parents to fully inform them of the sexual history and the details of his or her abusive behavior. The parents need to fully understand how the sexual acting-out occurred in order to take appropriate steps to establish new prevention rules at home.

4. The parents explore their marital relationship and other family dynamics in an effort to correct dysfunctional and unproductive patterns of behavior within the family unit.

5. The youth takes a polygraph examination to support and verify that his or her sexual history is complete. As noted earlier, polygraphs are not used with children under age 12. *Note:* Where polygraphs are not used, group therapy can be a good substitute in encouraging clients to be honest.

6. The child or adolescent begins the victim clarification process to ensure that all offending dynamics are explained and that any discrepancies in his or her reports are resolved. The youth continues to make good progress in specialized counseling.

7. The youth writes a clarification letter to the victim and to the victim's parents.

8. The youth reviews the letter with his or her therapist and the treatment group. The youth rewrites the letter as many times as needed until the letter contains no thinking errors, until it clearly and completely explains the offending dynamics, and until the therapist and treatment group have approved it. The letter is then sent to the victim's therapist, who reviews it and makes any recommendations for changes or suggests that the letter is ready to be shared with the victim.

Continued on next page

9. If the victim's therapist agrees, the offending young person will meet with the victim and the victim's therapist for the clarification process. In that meeting, those involved will begin developing house rules to protect the victim and to keep the offending youth from having opportunities to reoffend.

10. The youth meets with his or her parents and the victim (if appropriate and if approved) to discuss treatment progress and to establish house rules. The youth must be demonstrating honest, responsible, and healthy behavior at his or her residence, at school, and in treatment.

11. The youth is approved for brief visits with his or her parents (or the victim's parents, if different) and with younger children (including the victim) in neutral sites away from home (such as a restaurant, park, or some other place where the victim feels comfortable).

12. The offending youth's counselor consults with both the victim's therapist and the parents to review the process and to determine whether all parties are sticking to agreed-upon rules.

13. If possible, the youth's therapist or probation officer completes a home visit. When home visits are not practical or advised, it is helpful if the parents can provide the counselor with some pictures of the inside and outside of the house. This eyes-on perspective can be very helpful when the counselor is in the process of developing rules for the young offender's visits home. For example, seeing a picture of the living-dining-kitchen area can be important when discussing how a parent will supervise the youth and other children while a parent is preparing meals, bathing, and so forth.

14. Longer, outside-the-home visits are approved for the offending youth and his or her parents and siblings.

15. Brief, daytime, in-home visits are approved for the youth and for his or her parents and siblings.

16. One-night, overnight home visits are approved as long as the offending youth makes good treatment progress.

17. The young abuser continues to make good treatment progress. Additional polygraph tests support and verify his or her self-report about arousal patterns and behavior with the victim.

18. Parents continue to show solid commitment to the treatment process and to stay fully involved in the treatment of both the offending young person and the victim.

19. Longer, overnight visits are approved, leading to the young offender being able to move home on a full-time basis.

20. Full reunification occurs. The young offender remains in therapy for a significant period to monitor such things as his or her arousal and fantasy issues and adherence to house rules.

21. Periodic meetings are held with the victim's therapist and all family members to monitor the home environment and the client's behavior.

Following is a sample list of house rules that may be used when the abuser and the victim live in the same home. *Note:* While some of the rules listed below may apply to the victim and to other family members as well as to the client, they do not imply that the victim is responsible for any part of the client's abusive or inappropriate behavior. To establish appropriate boundaries in families where abuse has occurred, all members of the family must accept some "dress code" and "respect-for-space" rules.

- As the reunification process proceeds, the young abuser and the victim should each be in therapy with a (different) skilled specialist.
- Home visits are often helpful so that the individual therapists can identify potential supervision problems early on.
- There is no substitute for good visual supervision by a responsible adult who has been involved in the children's therapy process. Most reoffenses happen when children are allowed to play together or be in the house together without supervision.
- Door locks, door alarms, and video monitors can sometimes be helpful in maximizing supervision in a home. Room changes should also be considered so that a young abuser's bedroom is not located next to a vulnerable person's room or too far away from the household's adults. Inexpensive motion-triggered door alarms can be purchased at electronics supply stores such as Radio Shack. If a family decides to use an alarm, it is usually placed outside the young abuser's door. Sometimes a victim sleeps better if his or her door has an alarm (on the inside), too. Because of safety concerns, locks are of limited usefulness. If a client's behaviors or a victim's fears are so persistent that parents feel the need to lock the client in at night, placement at home should be reevaluated. Another

option is to use intercoms (look for "baby monitors" in stores) that enable parents to hear what's happening and allow a client to request permission for a bathroom visit.

- Bathroom doors should have locks, and family members should use them.
- The client should always bathe alone, not with siblings.
- The client, the victim, and the family should continue in therapy for an extended period after reunification, to ensure that boundaries and rules within the home are not slipping. It's all too common for parents to relax their guard after a few months of strict vigilance and no problems.
- Access to the Internet should be closely controlled and supervised. Clients who seek out pornography often experience drastic increases in sexual arousal and urges when viewing pornography, which can then lead to a reoffense.
- All cable television and satellite boxes should be equipped with parental locks, and clients should not have access to the code. Equipment should be set so that adult-oriented materials require a parental code, which is never shared with any of the children.
- All pornography and sexually explicit materials should be removed from the home. If such items are in the house, your kids can (and very often will) find them.
- Some control should be exercised over music with parental advisory notices on them. Sometimes it is just easier to have a blanket rule that any tape, CD, or MP3 with a parental advisory notice is not allowed in the house.

The following list of home rules was put together by one family for their 13-year-old son, Daniel, who had victimized his brother, Mark, who was five years younger than Daniel.

Our Family Rules for Visitation, Overnight Visits, and Reunification

1. Daniel should never be alone with children more than 24 months younger than he is. An approved chaperone needs to be in direct sight. (The allowable age difference for playmates can range from 12 to 36 months, depending on the client's age, history, and risk assessment.)
2. Bedroom and bathroom door locks will be working and will be used.
3. Goodnight hugs and other physical affection between Mark and Daniel are only to be initiated by Mark (who will never be pressured into such displays), not by Daniel.
4. All family members must be fully dressed in normal clothing or modest sleeping attire (no being in public areas in underwear) when in the common living areas or when going to or coming from the bathroom.
5. Daniel must sleep separately from other children.
6. When possible, Daniel will avoid sitting directly next to Mark or other younger children and will maintain some distance from Mark and other vulnerable people at home and in public (such as when watching television or sitting in the car).
7. Daniel will not have any child sit on his lap.
8. Wrestling or physical play with younger children is not allowed, unless directly supervised by an adult who has been involved in Daniel's treatment and his therapist has approved this type of contact. Grabbing, wrestling, touching, hitting, pushing, and tickling are not allowed.
9. No discussion will be held with siblings (Mark, Laura, and Shelly) about the abuse or treatment without a therapist present. Parents may ask questions about the treatment process or discuss the rules with the therapist.
10. Daniel and Mark will never be alone in the house or in a room together. If a parent or another approved chaperone is not home when Daniel arrives home, Daniel will remain outside the house if Mark is already home. Daniel will leave the house if he arrives before Mark does and no chaperone or parent is present when Mark arrives.
11. Daniel and Mark will both respect the personal boundaries of the other. This means not using the personal belongings of the other, not asking personal questions, and not verbally abusing the other.
12. Daniel is not to tell Mark what to do. Family members will not put Daniel in a position of authority over Mark or over any other household members or guests.
13. Daniel is never to enter Mark's bedroom, and Mark will never enter Daniel's bedroom. Exceptions may be made only when a parent is actually present in the room.
14. Normally, discipline of a younger child will be done only by the parent. Daniel will tell his parents or a chaperone when a younger child is misbehaving.
15. Add other rules here:

_____

_____

Signatures: _____   Date: _____

_____   _____

_____   _____

_____   _____

Some of these rules may not be appropriate for your family's situation, but they can serve as a starting point when establishing guidelines for a sibling-abuse situation.

This list of rules is an example only. The actual rules developed for your household will depend on the severity of your child's sexual behavior, the layout of the home, and the ages of the client and the victim. All rules should be discussed thoroughly with the client, victim, parents, and victim's therapist. The rules may change as circumstances in the home change or as the client's or victim's behavior changes. Any changes must be made in writing and only with the therapist's permission.

In all cases, it is the responsibility of the client to go out of his or her way to ensure the safety of the victim, even when an action is not required or is prohibited by the rules. For example, a client can grab a younger sibling victim to keep him or her from falling down a staircase. Clients need to be encouraged to use common sense in following their rules.

Following is a list of legal guidelines that govern adolescent and adult clients in Washington State. They are provided to give you some idea of how treatment providers and parents need to make cautious and careful decisions about the contact they allow between clients and vulnerable people.

1. Consider the victim's wishes about contact and ensure that all contact is safe and in accordance with any court directives.

2. Limit the client's decision-making authority over vulnerable children.

3. When the client has any contact with victims or children, the treatment provider will:
   a. Collaborate with other relevant professionals and solicit their input regarding contact with victims rather than make isolated decisions.
   b. Consult with parents, custodial parents, or guardians of vulnerable people prior to authorizing any contact between offending clients and children.
   c. Recognize that supervision during contact with children is critical for those clients who have offended against children or who have the potential to abuse children.
   d. Include educational experiences for chaperones or supervisors of clients.
   e. Establish a plan or protocol for reuniting or returning clients to homes where children reside. The plan needs to emphasize child safety.

Failure to follow these standards of practice can result in a treatment provider losing his or her license to practice or even in a parent or treatment provider being named in a lawsuit if a child is abused and the standards have not been followed.

Chapter 9

Making the Treatment Work through Good Supervision

The goal of supervision requirements is to prevent any further opportunities for sexual abuse, regardless of how low-risk or motivated for treatment the client may be. Treatment professionals agree that for adolescents with sexual behavior problems, some general supervision guidelines are widely accepted. For the adolescent who engages in sexual misconduct against young children, the following suggested rules should be adapted for the specific adolescent's family:

- No babysitting under any circumstances
- No access to young children or potential victims without direct supervision by a responsible adult who is aware of the problem
- No authority or supervisory role over young children (e.g., in school, church, or job activities)
- No possession or use of sexually explicit, "X-rated," or pornographic materials

It should be noted that rules do not preclude most ordinary daily activities, such as going to school, church, stores, or restaurants with the family, or involvement in age-appropriate and appropriately supervised peer activities. Although a number of safety and supervision issues need to be addressed with this population, it is crucial to remember that children and adolescents with sexual behavior problems are different from adult sex offenders. It may be helpful to review the information provided by the National Center on Sexual Behavior of Youth (www.ncsby.org) for further information about current trends and research on children and adolescents with sexual behavior problems.

Most juvenile court probation and parole orders require that a teenage sex offender not be alone with any child more than two or three years younger than the client. The orders usually specify no contact between the client and one or more younger children without the direct visual supervision of an adult who knows the youth's sexual behavior history.

The goal in most treatment programs is to help clients and families set up a community support network to help with supervision. Selected responsible adults in the community are educated about a client's sexual misbehavior, trained to look for certain specific warning signs, and taught about specific treatment rules. These people are often called *chaperones*. Chaperones are usually at least 21 years old, although in some cases people as young as 17 or 18 have been approved as chaperones in limited situations. A chaperone is told about the offender's behavior in enough detail to understand what happened and how seriously it has affected the family. A chaperone must be willing to sign a formal statement of responsibility and should at least have telephone contact with the treatment provider before being approved. A chaperone should be a responsible adult who does not have a criminal history or a history of inappropriate sexual behavior or substance abuse.

In this chapter you will find a list of general situations in which a chaperone is required, as well as a sample form you can adapt with your child's treatment provider to document approval of a specific adult as a chaperone. This chaperone approval process might sound somewhat intimidating and unnecessary. However, by using the suggested process, you are supporting your child's compliance with probation and parole orders. At the same time, you are establishing a positive community network where your child does not have to keep secrets and can get ongoing support for treatment efforts. One 13-year-old boy had 10 approved chaperones before he went to court to be sentenced for his sexual misconduct. This proactive support network certainly did not hurt his case when the judge was considering whether he was too dangerous to remain in the community. That youth received probation and was allowed to participate in community-based treatment.

The chaperone process is not just for youths on probation or parole. It is a good idea to use the process—even if no criminal charges are anticipated—to help reduce your child's risk of engaging in further sexual misconduct and to protect your child against future court sanctions. Using chaperones also helps protect you against potential negligence lawsuits, since you may be held accountable in a civil lawsuit for any sexual abuse your child perpetrates. The better the supervision you provide, the lower the chances of your child performing further sexual misconduct (which is how external barriers work).

It's not easy for parents to carry out the chaperone process because of the stigma, shame, fear, and embarrassment that go with disclosing their child's sexual behavior problem. A fine line exists between giving enough people enough information to ensure good supervision and respecting your child's privacy. Every decision to inform others should be carefully evaluated. Experience has shown that, in general, other people tend to be more supportive than most young people or their parents think they will be.

Guidelines for Using Approved Chaperones

The following guidelines are only general. Your child may require a lower or higher level of super-

vision than these generic procedures. Your child's treatment provider and probation or parole officer should make a case-specific determination. Chaperone training is needed:

1. For all parents or guardians of clients with sexual behavior problems, and
2. For all adults responsible for supervising and/or caring for children or adolescents with sexual behavior problems especially for significant periods of time, such as overnights.

A chaperone is needed:

1. Any time your child will be visiting a friend's or relative's home where younger children reside. (Nobody but the younger children's parents have the right to decide whether they wish to be around a person with sexual behavior problems.)
2. Any time your child will be going to an activity where extended unsupervised contact with children may occur (such as daytime or sleep-over camps or playgrounds where younger children will be present). The responsible adult should agree to be a chaperone and should go through the approval process with the treatment provider.
3. When your child holds a job that might involve periodic contact with children or some degree of responsibility for children. Your child's job supervisor may need to agree to be a chaperone. Most routine jobs not involving responsibility for children do not require a formal chaperone.
4. For clients who have abused drugs or alcohol or whose sexual behavior problems involve coercive, peer-age sexual behavior.
5. For certain social activities in the community.

A chaperone is not needed:

1. For your child to attend school with peers. If the school has day care in it, or if the school includes children more than three years younger than your child, however, special rules may apply.
2. For your child to go to a same-age friend's house where no younger children reside and where parental supervision is adequate.
3. For normal peer-age dating (movies, bowling, and the like). Adolescents with peer-age victims or predatory behavior such as exhibitionism may need special chaperone rules that involve more stringent supervision.
4. For normal adolescent work environments (such as fast-food restaurants or grocery stores).
5. For peer-oriented activities with same-age youth where unsupervised contact with younger children or vulnerable people is not likely to occur.

The chaperone approval form on the next page can be copied for use with different chaperones. Consult with your child's treatment provider for instructions about how to use this document.

Note to Chaperones

Please review the client's treatment rules to make sure that you fully understand the expectations of the client's treatment program. While most youth become committed to the treatment process, any of them can fall into old patterns of behavior that can be harmful if not interrupted. It is the chaperone's job to monitor for such old patterns of behavior and to encourage positive behavior change.

Youth who are falling into old patterns of behavior sometimes attempt to minimize the importance of their probation, parole, or treatment rules or any violations or infractions. Following is a list of some ways they might try to do this:

1. A child or adolescent might say that it is an exceptional circumstance, so the rule can be ignored. Note that if this is true, written authorization needs to be provided.
2. The young person might claim that he or she has no problem in a certain area and that they can handle the situation. If this is true, the treatment professional should provide written authorization.
3. These young people may claim that the rule simply doesn't apply to them. If this is true, the therapist needs to provide a written note to that effect.
4. Youth may claim that they are approaching the end of treatment, so they need not follow all the rules. If this is true, written authorization from the therapist must be provided. For the record, being near the end of treatment does not mean that rules can be ignored. On the contrary, being near the end of treatment means that rules are followed independently and that less monitoring and fewer reminders should be necessary.

When any question arises about any rule, please contact the therapist for clarification. In the meantime, assume that the rule is in effect. It is also appropriate to ask the client for the treatment provider's signature authorizing any change. If a chaperone observes a rule violation, it often works best if the chaperone asks the young person to report the violation to his or her treatment provider. The treatment provider can then contact the chaperone to discuss the violation and confirm that the youth reported the problem behavior. If the chaperone gets no call from the treatment provider, it must be assumed that the youth did not report the problem behavior. In that case, the chaperone should then call the treatment provider. This procedure puts the obligation on the young person to take responsibility for his or her behavior, and it helps chaperones to feel

Responsibility Statement for Approved Chaperones

In order to be approved as a chaperone, I have been informed of

_____ 's history of sexual offending and/or problem

sexual behavior. This person's specific problem behaviors include:

_____

_____

I have been informed of this client's probation/parole and/or treatment rules. I understand that any unsupervised contact with children more than two to three years younger than the client (or others who may be vulnerable to manipulation or force) may place those children at risk. I also understand that although this client is involved in and may be doing well in treatment, a reoffense is possible. High-risk situations for this client include, but are not limited to:

_____

I understand that supervising a person with sexual problems carries a certain responsibility and risk. As a chaperone approved to supervise _____ , I understand that my failure to report suspected rule violations committed by this client may leave me open to civil liability. I agree to report any obvious or suspected rule violations to _____ , the client's primary therapist, or to the police or children's protective services within 24 hours of the occurrence of the violation or suspected violation. I have also been informed of ways in which this client may attempt to manipulate me into minimizing the importance of the probation, parole, and/or treatment rules.

I understand that I am approved to chaperone this client in the following specific types of situations:

_____

_____

Chaperone's signature: _____ Date: _____

Chaperone's name (print): _____

Address: _____

City: _____ State: _____

Phone: _____

Client's signature: _____ Date: _____

Therapist's signature: _____ Date: _____

like they are not going behind their clients' backs to report such behavior.

Client Safety and Supervision Plans

Treatment programs, probation and parole officers, and the state Department of Social Services may require that your child have an approved safety or supervision plan to which everyone involved in the case agrees. At the end of this chapter there is an outline of a sample plan that you can take to your child's treatment provider in order to develop an initial supervision plan. Remember, as the parent of a child or adolescent with a sexual behavior problem, you are expected to strictly enforce the supervision plan. If you fail to enforce the plan, child protective services staff may find that other children in your home are at risk and take steps to remove them from your custody. If the plan is not enforced, the child with a sexual behavior problem may be placed in a residential treatment facility or a detention center. Please take this plan seriously; it is a very important part of the treatment and supervision process.

Consider the following true story of a boy who first received treatment for his sexual behavior problems when he was nine years old. The boy, an adopted child, was caught touching his younger sister, who was about age four at that time. The boy was referred to an outpatient clinic, where he received weekly counseling and education about sexuality. At age 11, the boy started sneaking across his hallway and going into his sister's bedroom and talking her into more sexual activity. He was then placed in a residential treatment center, where he received specialized counseling along with other children with sexual behavior problems. After two years, he had matured somewhat, and he was released from the residential facility and placed with his adoptive father, who had since divorced his adoptive mother. The boy continued in outpatient counseling on a weekly basis.

After about a year, the boy, by then 14 years old, was having trouble in school and was not going home directly after school. Unfortunately, his adoptive father worked full-time, so supervision after school was inadequate. The boy had been having regular visits with his mother and the sister he abused, since completing the apology (clarification) process and was having successful visits. The decision was then made to have the boy move in with his adoptive mother and sister. His mother was not working, so she was available to provide supervision. In addition, the mother had taken her 14-year-old niece into her home, so there was another person who was roughly the same age as the boy.

The boy and his family, including his sister and niece, continued in outpatient therapy for two more years, and he finally graduated from treatment at age 16. At that time he was given an aftercare plan that delineated recommended rules he should follow. Those rules included not being alone in the same room as his sister unless a chaperone was present. About a year after graduating from the treatment program, the boy was caught looking underneath the bathroom door at his sister, who was showering. She immediately told her mother, who called the prior counselor and the Department of Social and Health Services. The boy was then arrested and placed in juvenile detention. He was subsequently charged with one count of voyeurism, which is a felony sex offense in his state.

This situation is very tragic, but it highlights some important concepts that parents should be aware of. It highlights that human beings maintain strong sexual drives throughout their lives, so parents need to be constantly vigilant about the potential for children to continue their sexual acting-out, even after completing treatment. The sex drive is a lot like the drive to eat. Both sex and food are a necessary and ongoing part of human existence.

For those of you who have tried dieting, you will understand the dilemma. The urge to eat is noticeable each and every day. Each and every day we have to carefully choose what we eat, how much we eat, and how much exercise we will do to consume some of the calories we have eaten. With sexuality, we all face sexual feelings each and every day and daily have to make decisions about how we cope with those sexual desires.

In this boy's case, several factors seemed to be important in his relapse process. First, his cousin moved back in with her mother two months before his voyeurism incident, leaving him with one less person in the home, one less set of eyes, and more alone time with his sister. Also, he had broken up with his girlfriend, and he was again struggling with his schoolwork, both of which lowered his self-esteem. He reported that he started having sexual thoughts toward his sister, but thought he could handle them. So he did not choose to tell his mother or his previous counselor. Also, the rules and boundaries in the home began to erode, as his sister was gaining trust in him. She was now comfortable sitting on the same couch with him. In fact, she at times would put her legs in his lap, which was innocent and trusting in her mind, but the boy sometimes experienced sexual arousal when she did that. His mother allowed those changes to happen because by that time it had been *almost six years* since he had last acted out sexually. He had "graduated" from his counseling program, so in his distorted thinking, he thought that he would be letting his parents down by admitting to having new sexual thoughts about his sister. Complicating matters further, this boy had always been very quiet, and had always had a very hard time communicating his feelings. The boy had started masturbating to thoughts of his sister, but he kept telling himself that as long as he didn't act on those thoughts he would be okay. In the end, that distorted thinking was a significant factor in him becoming a sexual offender, which many people had tried to help him avoid during the years since his first incident of sexual acting-out.

So, let's review the key things that we can hope to learn from this family's tragedy:

- Aftercare rules, or *external barriers*, need to be maintained indefinitely. Think of it in a similar way to developing healthy eating habits in lieu of constant dieting. Once you stop dieting you soon regain the weight you had lost. The approach that will work better will be the establishment of a lifelong, healthy lifestyle of the right food intake and exercise. The same is true when you want to help children and adolescents who have sexual behavior problems. Throughout that help, be sensitive to the fact that all rules tend to erode over time.
- Children and adolescents need to be counseled and reminded to prepare for recurrent sexual feelings of an inappropriate nature. They are going to have sexual feelings. Parents need to help children and adolescents understand that they should feel no shame about having or communicating such feelings. The shame comes from acting on those sexual feelings in illegal or hurtful ways.
- Communicating feelings is very, very important. Had this boy been able to tell his mother or previous counselor that he was struggling with sexual feelings toward his sister, new supports could have been established that might have prevented his sexual reoffense.

Sexual acting-out can happen at any time. Going five or more years without a sexual behavior problem doesn't necessarily mean that a reoffense is not possible. Multiple factors can trigger further sexual acting-out, including obvious factors such as pornography use, drug use, or major life stressors such as depression, rejection, or some other failure experience.

Portions of this chapter are based on original material developed by Mary Meinig, M.S.W., and Benjamin Saunders, Ph.D. The author expresses his appreciation for their work in this field.

General Supervision Guidelines for Parents, Foster Parents, Group Home or Institution Staff, and Other Caregivers

1. Maintain bedroom privacy, for both adults and kids. It is usually a good idea for parents to keep their own bedroom private. Children should be expected to knock on all bedroom doors before entering.

2. Be cautious about touch and sexual contact. Some seemingly innocent touch can be sexually stimulating to children with sexual behavior problems. Some touch is important, however. Teach children to ask before touching you or others, and show respect for such boundaries by asking before touching them. This guideline may seem overly formal at first, but it is surprising how quickly you can learn to ask sincerely, "Can I give you a hug?"

3. Know where the child is at all times.

4. Have a reasonable understanding of travel times between destinations. Ask your child to account for all excessive time in getting to or from a destination. Be prepared for thinking errors and dishonesty. Always report such information to the child's therapist.

5. Know your child's friends. Always have the friend spend time at your house before allowing the child to go to a friend's house. Go visit the friend's home before you allow your child to visit there.

6. Learn about your child's friend's family. Find out who lives in the friend's home, and inquire specifically about younger siblings and relatives. If victim-age children live there, and if the friend's parents are responsible and you think visits to the friend's home are appropriate, prohibit any visits until the parents complete the chaperone approval process. Ask yourself, would you want a sex offender visiting in your home without you knowing about it?

7. If your child is at a friend's house, feel free to call and see what he or she is doing. Don't worry about violating trust. You are showing that you love your child and that you care about his or her success. Remember that trust can be abused; good supervision cannot be.

8. Do not allow your child to babysit or care for younger children.

9. When asking about your child's activities, do not ask yes or no questions; they encourage denial. Instead of asking, "Did you go anywhere else?" ask, "Where else did you go?"

10. When you doubt what your child is telling you, write down your concerns to share with the therapist later.

11. If your child is having any kind of behavior problem at school, consider requesting a meeting with teachers and counselors to share information. Ask teachers to send periodic feedback home or to call home if problem behavior is noted.

12. Don't allow your child to wrestle, tickle, or engage in sports involving excessive physical contact with younger children.

A Young Person's Safety and Supervision Plan

Youth's name: _____ Date of plan: _____

Note: Treatment provider should initial and date
changes on the list when they are made.

1. Client **may / may not** be alone in the home/foster home.

   If yes, this young person may be home alone for periods of up to _____ hours.

2. Client **may / may not** have community access alone.

   If yes, specify where client may go: _____

3. Client **may / may not** walk to school alone.

4. Client **may / may not** not take public transportation (bus, subway, etc.) alone.

5. Client **may / may not** take the bus to school alone.

6. Client **needs / doesn't need** an aide at school to supervise between classes, at lunch, or at recess.

7. Client **may / may not** use the usual rest room at school.
   If not, develop a special plan with the school.

8. Client **may / may not** participate in school or league sports without supervision by a parent or chaperone.

9. Client **may / may not** go on school field trips or other school activities without a chaperone.

10. Client **may / may not** go to movies with peer-age friends without an approved chaperone.

11. Client **may / may not** have peer-age friends spend the night.

12. Client **may / may not** visit friends at their homes without a chaperone.

13. Client **may / may not** spend the night at friends' homes where no younger children are present.

14. Client **may / may not** play in his or her front yard without direct supervision.

15. Client **may / may not** play in his or her backyard without direct supervision.

16. Client **requires / does not require** constant visual supervision when outside.

17. Client **requires / does not require** constant visual supervision whenever other children are present.

18. Client **may / may not** hold a job. Appropriate types of jobs include:

_____

Continued on next page

19. Client **will / will not** have a door alarm installed on the bedroom door.

20. Client **may** use the Internet at all times without restriction; client **may not** ever use the Internet; client **may** use Internet at home with parental supervision; client **may** use Internet at school with supervision; client **may** use Internet at school without supervision. (Circle all that apply.)

21. Client may view television/videos rated: **G, PG, PG-13, or R.**
    (Circle all that apply, and specify who is approved to make exceptions.)

22. Client may play video games rated: **E, T, MA, A, none.** (Circle all that apply.)

23. Client **may / may not** possess audiotapes, CDs, or digital music files with parental advisory warnings.

24. Client **may / may not** share a bedroom with another child.

    If yes, specify age and gender of allowed roommates: _____

25. Client **may / may not** use a telephone without supervision.

26. Other rules:

    _____

    _____

    _____

Date last revised: _____

Names of approved chaperones: _____

Signatures:

    Client: _____

    Parent: _____

    Therapist: _____

    Other: _____

Chapter 10

What Now? When Is This Problem Over?

If your child has developed a sexual behavior problem at a young age and does not have other complicating mental health or behavior problems, it is very possible that the actual counseling and treatment process will be relatively short. It is very important, however, to understand that sexual feelings and urges are lifelong, and that children who have developed sexualized behaviors will likely not be able to stop their sexual feelings or may forget what they have learned about their sexual responses. Therefore, parental supervision, support, and involvement are often key factors in a child's future success. It is important to also understand that sexual feelings and urges almost always intensify significantly during puberty. Close supervision and parental involvement is very important during the years that a child is experiencing pubertal changes. As noted earlier in this book, sexual behavior problems and sexual abuse within families can often be the result of many different, complex factors. Correcting all of the factors that resulted in the sexual abuse can be a daunting task.

Consider the life story that Todd wrote as part of his treatment and has offered to share with you below. Todd sexually abused his younger sister when he was between the ages of 9 and 16. His story illustrates the complexity of sexual acting-out in families and points out that many other patterns of behavior are connected to the sexual offending. Todd completed all treatment requirements during the more than two years he was involved in an outpatient treatment program.

Most of my childhood is still a blur to me. I do remember an incident of being a victim. I was left alone with a girl who took care of me and I would always find myself in her bed, and I would stay the night with her in a bed. I don't remember much about what happened. The girl was my babysitter, and I think what happened with her had a lot to do with my future behaviors. She was probably a teenager, and she was the daughter of my parents' friends.

I remember meeting a girl in the first grade who told me that she had had sex with people. I remember talking to her at recess. Before that, though, I had been having some sex dreams in kindergarten. Sometime during elementary school, I remember one girl telling my older brother, who is three years older than me, that she wanted his body. This sticks out in my mind, because I didn't know what she meant—but I wanted to. I remember her talking to him over some fence, and it made a permanent implant in my head.

My older brother was always mean to me. He picked on me, and always hit me. He just wasn't nice to me. He started me on drinking and smoking pot when I was about 13 years old. I was a little pyro back then, during elementary school. I didn't burn anything down; I just liked to play with fire. It was a great prize to find a lighter that worked. I loved the Fourth of July, and I would save up all of my money to buy fireworks (when firecrackers were legal). It was fun to blow things up.

I was nine years old when I started abusing my sister. She was three years old. I remember taking her into the furnace room, where my dad's study was. I remember taking her clothes off, and I took mine off, too. I did not know how to have sex, and I was very clumsy and ended up poking at her with my penis, but not knowing what to do.

It started with me fondling her and touching her. It didn't happen very much at first. As I got older it changed into more oral sex and masturbation. I would go through cycles. Sometimes I would be uncontrollably horny, and I would wait for her to get home from school. I would plan what I would say to her and how to bribe her. I never used force. I would offer her money or candy, and I would do her chores for her. I would always try to make the deal as sweet as possible for her. I was doing all kinds of things for her. I would do almost everything she asked, except stop. Sometimes I would stop abusing her for a while, like a few months. But I always went back to abusing her again. Sometimes I had no urges at all, and I would almost forget about it. I started having girlfriends in the eighth grade, when I was 14. When I had girlfriends I didn't do anything with my sister. I always had to get off, and it helped to have a girlfriend. It was like an addiction; I always had to get off. I have no way of knowing how much I abused her, but it went on until I was 16 years old, so there were more incidents than I can count.

I stopped abusing my sister sometime after the first time I had sex with a girlfriend. About a year later my sister told my mom about my abuse. She broke down one night and told our mom everything. My mom and dad called me into their room and told me that she had told them everything. I was 17 years old at that time. My parents asked me if it was true. I broke down crying and admitted to everything. It was a relief, and I knew that what I had done was wrong. My dad was seeing a counselor at that time, and he told the counselor about it. The counselor reported my abuse to Children's Protective Services, and later on my dad was called by the police and asked to deliver me to the police station. I went to the police interview and admitted everything I had done. After that I started seeing a counselor. Sometimes I would see him after spending the night partying. I finally stopped partying when another counselor told me I would go to jail if I didn't stop using drugs and alcohol. I remember that I was pissed back then, because I didn't want to stop using drugs.

I always knew that some kind of discovery of my behavior was coming. Any time my parents called me into their room to talk with me, I was afraid that my sister had told on me. I was always nervous that my parents were going to find out. It was actually kind of a relief when she told, because the whole thing had been building inside me. I was really stressed about it. I knew that what I was doing was wrong. I had been using a lot of drugs and alcohol to get my mind off of it. I was always partying, frying my mind. Now I see it as "escapism." If I wasn't doing drugs, I was reading. I would read and put my mind into another world to get away.

At home during this time it was hell. My dad hated me, because he had been molested as a kid, and it brought back all those feelings. My mother was torn between my sister and me. My older brother hated me and wanted to kill me. He punched a hole in my wall. My younger brother was aloof and avoided dealing with me. I hated being home, and I would use any excuse to get out of the house. I avoided my sister, and she seemed to be upset with herself because she thought I would hate her for life. She cried about that for a long time with my mom. She was upset at herself. Even though she told on me and wanted it to be known, she didn't want everything that happened to happen. I had told her when I was abusing her that if she told, the whole family would be ripped apart. And that is exactly what ended up happening.

Things really got better after I got back from jail and was on probation. I spent 30 days in jail after court. It was weird coming home. My life had already changed, and I had lost all motivation for anything. I spent a lot of time sitting around, trying to figure out what to do. I was told that I had to get a job or go to school full-time, so I found a job and started working. My sister was glad to have me come home, and she had even visited me in jail. It was weird, seeing her there. I think she had already forgiven me. She started counseling about the same time I did. She is very smart and talented. She is a 4.0 (grade-point average, equivalent to straight A's) student, and she is an excellent piano player. We are a lot alike; we are both very artistic.

Going to counseling has helped me be more open about what I have done. I had no trouble telling my group what I did, but it made it a lot easier after I did tell them. I have already told five people outside my family about my offenses. They were understanding and I still talk to them. Nobody acts differently toward me, and I didn't have any negative reactions from anyone I told. My best friend had a very positive reaction when I told him. He gave me a hug and said he was sorry. He understood what I was going through.

I have one major rule at home in order to help my sister feel safe, and for me to maintain good boundaries. I can't be in the home alone with my sister, and if she is home I need to be in a place that can be easily supervised. I usually stay in one divided half of the house. I read, and she usually watches TV in the other side of the house. Other than that, things at home are pretty normal. In the beginning of my treatment we came up with many other new

rules that we still follow. For example, at first we decided that neither of us goes into the other's room. We have been getting along pretty good; we don't argue or fight. When I talked to her and apologized directly for my abuse of her, she told me that she wanted to forgive me as long as I followed my rules. She doesn't consider me a threat anymore, and I know I'm not a threat anymore. I plan to continue following all of my treatment rules so that there is no chance of a relapse.

As I have progressed more in treatment I have come to realize how I used to control and manipulate my sister excessively. It wasn't just my sister. I used it in my everyday life with my parents as well as my girlfriends. I would always have to get my way, and I would make sure I got my way by hounding them, being subtle about what I said. I would change what they said into a different context. For example, if they admitted liking something, I would change it to something I wanted. If someone gave me the slightest clue that they liked something, I would convince them to do what I wanted, all the while convincing them it was something they wanted. If it wasn't something they wanted, it was something they came to expect. I was conditioning people. With my parents it was harder, but I would nag them and change the subject so that they would agree with what I was saying. Once in a while I would try to confuse people by saying I didn't want to do it. For example, I would work at my sister to get her to agree to have oral sex with me. Then I would say I didn't want to do it. Then I would later bring it up and say, "Remember when you agreed to do oral sex? Well, I want to do it now." Over a period of time it isn't even a struggle to get people to do what you want. They start to believe that this is the way that things are supposed to be. Back then I was using people quite extensively. From the moment I woke in the morning to the time I went to bed, I had to work hard to find ways to get people to do what I wanted. I was trying to control every little thing I could. It got very stressful to make sure that I didn't cross stories—that I kept my stories straight.

As the end of my treatment approaches, I find myself feeling a bit nervous and anxious about getting off probation and ending this treatment. I even lie awake at night, wondering about the great unknown that is rushing up to meet me. It's pleasant, but at the same time it scares me. I've grown accustomed to coming to my counselor's office every Friday. It will be different when I don't have him anymore. It's like being in a comfort zone now, and it is going to be hard to break out of. But it is something that has to be done, something I have to do. I have been told by a lot of people that I have finally grown up, and that I am acting responsible. I used to hate that word. I used to hate thinking of myself as a responsible individual. But it is a nice feeling now. I am glad that I am finally considered a responsible adult.

Update: Todd continued to maintain periodic telephone contact with his treatment program for several years. He reported that he had finished a two-year college program, majoring in art, and was successfully employed at a graphic-design firm. He was engaged to be married, and said he and his sister have developed a very healthy and positive relationship. His parents also reported that he has maintained his treatment gains.

This outcome is one of many examples of how a treatment process can result in positive long-term change and improvement in overall family functioning. Todd's story also illustrates how complex a sexual behavior problem can be and how other emotional, mental health, and family issues are often involved in the development of a sexual behavior problem.

If your child is an adolescent and has participated in a treatment program, the counselor will likely be able to give some recommendations about what the client should or should not do in the years following completion of the treatment program. The majority of the professional therapeutic community agrees that children and adolescents with sexual behavior problems need to continue to pay attention to the boundaries and skills they have learned during the treatment process. What follows is an example of an aftercare plan that is used in one outpatient treatment program. The plan is individualized for each client based on their unique risk assessment, although some general principles guide each specific plan. After the plan is developed, the young person and his or her parents all sign the plan to ensure it will be supported following completion of treatment.

Aftercare Recommendations for Sexual Behavior Treatment

Client Name: _____ D.O.B. _____

Program Completion Date: _____ Client's age at discharge: _____

The following general recommendations are provided to help young people in a sexual behavior program maintain their treatment gains and avoid situations that could increase their risk of sexual acting-out. The young person as well as any involved caregivers and support people should be aware of these rules and that violations of these rules could lead to sexual acting-out or sexual offenses. A caregiver or support person who observes any behaviors on this list should discuss the issue with the young person and also discuss concerns with his or her parent or guardian. Consultation with a trained sexual behavior therapist should also be sought.

1. The client should never be given child care or babysitting responsibility for younger children. (An exception could be made for clients who care for their own biological children after several years of post-treatment success that was devoid of high-risk or illegal behaviors.)

2. The client should actively avoid ever being alone with younger children or with any other high-risk group (such as developmentally delayed people as indicated by the client's risk assessment).

3. The client should refrain from use of pornography, since pornography use nearly always increases sexual arousal and sexual interest.

4. The client should not engage in hands-on physical activities with younger children such as playing tag, wrestling, tickling, or touching. Such activities often lead to sexual arousal, and are one of the most frequent sources of arousal that lead to reoffending.

5. Alcohol and drug use are disinhibitors, and are illegal for clients under age 21. Drugs or alcohol are risk factors and do nothing but increase risk. Client should not use illegal drugs, and should only use alcohol when it is legal and responsible for him or her to do so.

6. Clients who do not actively avoid younger children, or who show a special interest in children, are demonstrating high-risk behavior. We expect clients to establish a polite but distant relationship with all younger children.

7. Clients who socialize with younger children, play with younger children, or date people more than two years younger than themselves are demonstrating high-risk behavior.

Continued on next page

8. Clients who experience recurrent sexual arousal, thoughts, or fantasies directed toward younger children are encouraged to immediately disclose those thoughts to their parents or other support people, and to seek additional counseling.

9. The client is expected to maintain appropriate physical boundaries with siblings, and to follow all previously agreed-upon family reunification rules.

We understand these guidelines, and understand that successful completion of treatment requires continued adherence to these guidelines.

_____   _____

Parents   Date

_____   _____

Client   Date

_____   _____

Therapist   Date

The Aftercare Process:
What Happens After Treatment Ends?

Even as your child nears completion of his or her treatment program, the treatment and supervision process goes on. If you are the parent of a child in a residential or institutional treatment program, it is important to understand that treatment is never completed in such a residential program. That is because residential and institutional programs are very artificial and do not adequately represent the stressors and temptations of real everyday life. Such programs are closely supervised and highly structured, making it easier for youth to make good choices and difficult for them to make poor choices. When a child or adolescent is released from a residential or institutional program, that is when treatment really begins, and youth then need to start actually using their newly learned skills to make real-life choices.

It is a mistake to think that when a child is released from a residential program they are "cured" and close supervision and support is not necessary. The opposite is actually true. Youth need a great deal of support and guidance when they reenter the community from such facilities. This usually means that they should be enrolled in an outpatient treatment program after they are released from a residential facility so that they can receive community-based support and assistance until they are well-established in a productive and healthy lifestyle.

As your child progresses enough to need less frequent aftercare treatment and supervision, he or she will take on more responsibility for personal decisions. With your help, your child will succeed in becoming a lifetime member of what we call the sexual abuse prevention and safety team by making decisions that lead away from offending and that help shape an adulthood free from problem sexual behavior. Many therapists are inspired by what is called the Good Lives Model of rehabilitation for people with sexual behavior problems. This model emphasizes the need for clients to not only decrease unhealthy behaviors, but also increase healthy aspects of their lives through participation in positive, growth-oriented activities.

Helping a child overcome a sexual behavior problem can be a daunting, demanding, and challenging task that can last for many years. One foster father who had been through three difficult years with his young foster/adopt son, has written about some of his thoughts about the process. To his credit, the caring and consistent parenting offered by these parents resulted in their child making dramatic improvements in severe sexual behavior problems.

Raising a child with serious sexual behavior problems presents unique challenges for parents. Most traditional parenting classes and training do not prepare parents for dealing with children with sexual behavior problems. Consider the experience of one 48-year-old teacher, who decided, along with his wife, to apply for a foster care license and take on parenting responsibilities for a six-year-old boy, who turned out to have very, very serious sexual behavior problems.

I am writing this because when your child is recognized as being sexually aggressive, all those books on parenting and adoption don't really help much. My foster child's name is Max, and he experienced substantial abuse and neglect as a young child, and he had been removed from several other homes due to his sexually aggressive behaviors with children and adults.

I have slowly realized that I have needed to re-invent myself into the parent Max needed, not the one I wanted to be. I thought back to the foster-adopt training that my wife and I went through in order to become licensed foster-adopt parents. They kept emphasizing that it wasn't about what we wanted, it was about what the child needed. I also remember explaining to Max's counselor what I perceived my parenting style to be, a combination of laid back and laissez-faire approaches to parenting that assumes that people learn best from making their own mistakes. Max's counselor frowned, and then told me his experience suggested that style doesn't work very well for these kids. It was clear that for Max to learn and change, I was going to have to learn and change too.

It's been almost threee years since Max moved into our home with my wife and I. I am a teacher by training, and now a father and farmer in training, spending almost all my free time nurturing and coaxing a neglected orchard back into productivity while restoring an old orange tractor and learning to ferment Asian pear juice. I have come to believe that these activities will help me provide wisdom, love, and discipline to the six-year-old foster child who arrived at my house with more behavioral labels and sexual problems than an angry pit bull in heat.

Max had been in weekly counseling with his specialized sexual behavior therapist for about 15 months when he admitted to stealing my 10 dollars to do "bad touch" on one of his community center friends. Words don't really describe the discouragement I felt. When he first arrived in our home Max was an unbridled bundle of sexual energy. He talked of wanting to have sex with me, my wife, and anything that moved. He would reach out to touch private parts whenever he got close enough to do so. After seeing some consistent, yet sporadic progress, it seemed as if we had revisited everything my wife and I worked so hard to prevent. I realized after Max stole that 10 dollars to do sexual touching we felt so personally devastated because we invested so much of ourselves in this process. His counselor told my wife and I that we shouldn't be too surprised that Max had done it again after such a long time showing restraint—after all, when he came into our

house he was trying to do it to me, or talking about it every day for the first three months. To have shown restraint for so long could be looked at as how far he has come.

My wife and I again reconsidered whether it still made sense to try to be Max's parents. It was then I realized how he had become more than just a strong part of my farming self, which I must admit to having an amazing amount of fun with. In truth, he is the impetus for these efforts. I have come to the recognition that I value the person I am becoming more than the person I am. I really can't have one without the other. When I am having a hard time valuing Max, I remember how much I value the person I am becoming and somehow I begin to think in a more kind way about the boy who lives in my house. My experience on my farm is at least equal, and honestly—some days it may not balance out in his favor. Yet perhaps all parents, if we were forced to be honest and insightful, would recognize our own value foibles when it comes to our children.

I sometimes worry I am losing something of myself in this 24/7 parenting job. Such intensive support for another human being invariably influences all people involved in the process. Am I losing myself, or am I expanding the definition of who I am to include and revisit values I have taken for granted? We never really know what we are taking for granted until we find it at risk. I watch with a mixture of loss and envy as other parent's children give them hugs without asking permission. Having to ration out, and sometimes deny physical affection to Max is so hard. He is a loving boy who craves attention, yet his sexual behavior support needs sometimes put a physical and emotional distance between us. Yes—this gap is slowly closing, but sometimes it hurts so much to have to put distance between yourself and your child.

Max is a ward of the state now—his biological parents signed away their rights. I now feel responsible for helping him. The state is trying to get my wife and I to sign the title to him (adoption), to become the ones responsible to try to straighten his bent life, to be the ones responsible when something breaks. We say we are "committed to Max" but what does that really mean?

My wife recently asked a child psychologist to define unconditional love. He told us about a foster child he had recently met. His foster parents were talking to him about being his forever family. Yet when the boy scratched his foster mom during a conflict, he was sent to live somewhere else because he broke the house rules. That, the doctor said, is conditional love. Unconditional love might be strict, even severe—but it provides the opportunity to learn from mistakes. Unconditional love is what forever families provide.

If everything goes according to the latest plan, Max will take our last names in a permanency hearing on his ninth birthday. That he wants to take our last names is impressive, though I'm not certain it is a prerequisite to permanency. Hell—my wife didn't even do that and my marriage has 23 years of permanency.

My wife and I are becoming a mom and dad. We are becoming a forever family. Max already calls us that. Becoming mom and dad involves more than a name. I think I would enjoy the chance to feel like I was Max's dad, but for the moment we are "in process," as the social workers call it. I am beginning to think that being Max's forever dad is going to mean being forever in this process of support with an elusive and shifting sense of success. From a distance, our family looks and functions like everyone else's, yet when we find ourselves raising a sexually aggressive child, the details define the experience, and every day brings new challenges, frustrations, and fortunately, successes.

Whenever a child or adolescent with sexual behavior problems successfully completes specialized early treatment, it means that many potential victims have been saved from a lifetime of trauma. Staying involved in the treatment process and providing good supervision after formal treatment ends are critical contributions you make to your child's success. Parents who have taken on this job and stayed with it despite the emotional storms and roller coasters have earned the respect of treatment providers throughout North America and elsewhere. We hope we can count on you to continue to be one of them.

Appendix

How to Support Your Child's Involvement in the *Roadmaps* and *Pathways* Workbooks

Note: This appendix is designed specifically to support clients who are using the Roadmaps *second-edition or the* Pathways *fourth-edition workbooks.*

If your child is working in the *Roadmaps* workbook, the final assignment is developing a comprehensive Safety Plan Book. This assignment often starts as soon as the client starts working in *Roadmaps* and it continues through the last chapter of that book. This personal Safety Plan Book is made when your child reviews what he or she is learning in *Roadmaps* and assembles the information into a three-ring notebook that will serve as a reminder of the treatment concepts he or she has learned. Your involvement in this process is very important. If your child is working in the *Pathways* fourth-edition workbook, he or she will be working for several months to develop a Healthy Living Project. You can support your child by giving ideas and helping your child organize the notebook that contains the Healthy Living Project.

The following lists provide you with a positive way to open the lines of communication and get involved in your child's work in the *Roadmaps* and *Pathways* workbooks. Remember, if your child is using other books or treatment materials, it is helpful if you look at and read those materials so that you can better support what your child is learning. You are encouraged to spend some time each week asking the questions that follow and talking about what your child is learning in the treatment process. By having these discussions, you are helping your child internalize treatment concepts, and you are showing positive support and encouragement for the treatment process.

If you or your child finds certain questions too intrusive, you may prefer to discuss them with your child's counselor.

Questions to Ask Your Child As Treatment Progresses If Your Child Is Using the *Roadmaps* Workbook

Note: If your child is working in Pathways, *skip ahead to the next section. If your child is working in another treatment workbook, become familiar with that material and ask your child questions about what he or she is learning.*

It may help the process if you tell your child that you also have a treatment assignment and treatment workbook. Explain to your child that your assignment is to ask the questions listed below and to give feedback on the child's answers. Explain to the child that it is important that parents learn about the things their children are learning. Ask your child what chapter he or she is working on in *Roadmaps*. That book contains a progress chart that children can mark or decorate after each chapter is completed. By showing an interest in the chart, you can support your child's enthusiasm for the treatment process. As each chapter is completed, set aside some private time to review the following questions with your child.

Chapter 1: Start Your Engines
1. Ask your child who Buzzbee is. Buzzbee is a supportive little car that serves as a guide. Buzzbee will give much helpful advice during your child's work in

99

Roadmaps. Say some nice things, for example, "Buzzbee sounds helpful and wise."

2. Chapter 1 contains a sharing exercise (one that is not about sexual behavior problems). Ask your child to share it with you. Feel free to give compliments or ask additional questions.

3. Assignment 1B asks children to draw a picture of themselves, their family members, and their homes. Ask to look at the pictures and praise your child's efforts. Ask your child to explain what is in the drawings.

4. Each chapter in *Roadmaps* contains a test at the end of each chapter. Ask your child if you may see the test. What your child has written will give you a chance to ask more questions to make sure your child really understands what is in the chapter. If you participate in this process, the learning experience will be far greater.

Chapter 2: What Is a Touching Problem?

1. Chapter 2 explains that sexual feelings can be very strong. The chapter offers suggestions for managing such feelings. Now would be a good time (and opportunity) to show your child that you are comfortable talking about sexual topics. You may want to give a personal example from your life about what healthy coping activities you did when you got strong sexual feelings as a child or teenager. But be sure you don't imply that you made smart decisions while your child didn't. A comparison that undermines or embarrasses your child will not teach the child to respond differently. It will only fill the child with shame.

2. Chapter 2 asks children to make a list of the people they can talk to about their sexual feelings. Ask if you can look at their list and confirm that it is good for them to talk with you, if you are on the list. If your name is not on the list, offer to be a person your child could talk with about sexual feelings. If your child agrees, ask your child to put your name on the list.

3. Ask your child what a sexual behavior problem is. *Roadmaps* defines a sexual behavior problem as when somebody touches someone else's private parts without permission or when the person being touched is too young to know what's going on.

4. Ask your child when sexual touching is bad. Also ask when sexual touching is good. *Roadmaps* explains that sexual touch of an age-appropriate person is good, if that person has given permission for the touching. But the book explains that sexual touch is not all right if you or the person you touch are too young or if the touching hurts, upsets, or bothers either person.

5. Ask your child what private parts are. *Roadmaps* defines private parts as a person's bottom, anus, chest, penis, vulva, and vagina. Praise your child for learning this definition.

6. Ask your child, "What is incest?" (Incest is intercourse or sexual touching between people in the same family, but not including sexual activity between a wife and husband or between other consenting adult partners.)

7. Ask your child for the name of the special place kids go when they get into trouble for wrong sexual touching. *Roadmaps* explains that children don't go to adult jails but to special jails or residences for children where they have to stay while they get help for their sexual problems. These places are also called kids' jail or juvenile detention (juvie).

8. Ask your child to explain what sexual harassment is. *Roadmaps* describes it as when a person says or does something sexual or personal that bothers another person.

9. Ask your child to provide an example of sexual harassment.

10. If your child is in a treatment group, ask about the group rules.

11. Chapter 2 asks each child to draw a picture of himself or herself. Ask your child if you may look at those pictures. Offer compliments and thank your child for sharing the drawings.

12. Chapter 2 contains a list of your child's problems and goals. Ask if you may look at the list and offer suggestions. Always make sure that you make a positive comment about your child's hard work on this assignment.

13. Ask to review the chapter 2 test with your child.

14. Congratulate your child on his or her hard work in chapter 2.

Chapter 3: Learning to Talk About My Feelings

1. This chapter asks children to talk about what makes them happy and angry. Ask your child to list some things that make him or her happy.

2. Ask what things make your child angry.

3. *Roadmaps* teaches that anger sometimes is the result of lots of other feelings, many of which are often not even apparent or visible. Therapists refer to this situation as the Anger Iceberg, where the feelings underneath the anger are below the surface. This analogy is important; 80 percent of an iceberg is below the surface of the water. Tell your child that it is important to think about what other feelings might be hidden out of sight when the child experiences being angry. Ask your child to show you the picture of the anger iceberg in *Roadmaps*.

4. Ask your child to name as many feeling words as possible. If your child has difficulty with this, help out by naming some other feelings. In coming weeks try to use as many feeling words as you can when you are interacting with your child. When your child gets mad, prompt him or her to talk about what other feelings are hidden underneath the anger.

5. *Roadmaps* teaches children about three types of behavior: passive, assertive, and aggressive. Ask your child for an example of each type of behavior. *Roadmaps* teaches that to be assertive people need to say how they feel and what they want. They won't always get what they want, but they should ask for it anyhow.

6. One of your child's assignments in *Roadmaps* is to practice being assertive three times this week. Try to support your child in doing this, and when you notice that he or she has been assertive, help your child write about it in the *Roadmaps* workbook (assignment 3H).

7. Ask your child to show you the road test for chapter 3. Congratulate your child for the hard work that was done in this chapter.

Chapter 4: Right Touching and Wrong Touching

1. Ask your child what right touching is.

2. Ask your child what it means when a behavior is legal. Make sure you reinforce the idea that even though something might be legal, it is not always smart, right, or appropriate.

3. Ask your child to explain what it means when a behavior is illegal.

4. Ask your child to explain what wrong touching is.

5. Ask your child to name some good reasons to stop doing wrong touching. This topic is from assignment 4A. Ask your child to check the *Roadmaps* workbook if he or she can't think of the reasons.

6. Ask your child what good things might happen if he or she stops all wrong touching.

7. Ask your child to give you the test, assignment 4B. Help your child read each item. Then you need to give the answer you think is best. Ask your child if he or she agrees, since the counselor should have already corrected his or her answers.

8. Ask your child to share what he or she wrote on assignment 4C, which asks him or her to name five examples of right touching he or she has done in the past.

9. Ask your child to share what he or she wrote on assignment 4D, which asks for five examples of wrong touching that your child has done in his or her lifetime.

10. Ask your child to show you the road test for chapter 4. Congratulate and praise your child for the hard work that was done in this chapter.

Chapter 5: Right Thinking and Wrong Thinking

1. In *Roadmaps*, your child is learning many new ways to alter behavior. One of the most important things your child is learning is how to *think* differently. When people pay close attention to how they are thinking and why they might be having those thoughts, they can learn to change their behavior.

2. Ask your child what right thinking leads to (such as right touching, healthy choices, and what eventually be a happy and successful life).

3. Ask your child what wrong thinking leads to (wrong touching and lots of problems).

4. Ask your child to name the thinking errors. They are:
   - Blaming
   - Minimizing
   - Lying
   - Lack of empathy
   - Anger
   - Excuse making
   - "Never; ever; always"

5. Ask your child to explain what each thinking error listed above means.

6. Ask your child to give you three examples of right thinking from the past week or two. You can suggest that your child look at assignment 5A to review what was written on that assignment.

7. Ask your child to review assignment 5B with you. If you feel up to it, ask your child to test you on each one. If your child agrees to do that, help him or her read the assignment and then guess which thinking error was being used in each instance. This exercise will put your child in the role of a teacher, which will increase his or her self-esteem and self-confidence.

8. Ask your child to explain the word *denial.*

9. Ask your child to review the list of things he or she has told the truth about in the past several months (assignment 5C).

10. Ask your child what self-talk is. Ask your child to review what he or she wrote in assignment 5D, which asks for a list of positive things that a person likes about himself or herself.

11. Ask your child to show you the road test for chapter 5. Congratulate and praise your child for the hard work that was done in this chapter.

Chapter 6: What Should I Do When I Get Sexual Feelings?

1. Ask your child what happens during puberty.

2. Ask your child if he or she should be ashamed of having sexual feelings. (The answer is no.) Reinforce the point that sexual feelings are not bad and make clear that everybody has such feelings and responses.

3. Ask your child what he or she has learned about masturbation. For example, your child has learned that boys and girls both masturbate sometimes but that masturbation should only be done in private.

4. Ask your child what a sexual urge is. *Roadmaps* teaches that a sexual urge is the desire to do some sexual touching or sexual behavior.

5. Ask your child to list some ways to control sexual urges.

6. Ask your child what he or she wrote in assignment 6A. If you are not on the list, tell your child that you would like to help him or her feel comfortable enough that he or she feels fine about having you on that list.

7. Ask your child to review what he or she wrote in assignment 6C, which is about ways to control sexual urges. Tell your child that you will work with him or her to help them use some of those methods.

8. Ask your child to show you the road test for chapter 6. Congratulate and praise your child for the hard work done in this chapter.

Chapter 7: Understanding and Caring for My Changing Body

1. Talk to your child about puberty. Ask what he or she has learned about the changes people's bodies go through during puberty.

2. Ask your child about what he or she has learned about circumcision.

3. Ask what else your child has learned about human bodies in this chapter. The chapter provides information about stages of puberty, menstruation, pregnancy, and male and female anatomy. Try to be as positive and supportive as you can, because if you show that you are comfortable with this discussion, your child will be more likely to confide in you later about sexual feelings, urges, and behaviors.

4. Ask your child to review assignment 7A. This assignment is about personal care and hygiene. Offer to help your child remember to work on the tasks on the list that he or she needs to work on.

5. Assignment 7B helps your child create a weekly behavior chart for practicing new, healthy behaviors. This chart will only work if you review it every day with your child and provide lots of praise and reinforcement. When you help your child pick goals to work on, start with easy ones that will likely be successful. You can always add harder ones later.

6. Tell your child that you are proud of all the positive and healthy things that he or she does to take care of his or her body. Give examples of what your child is doing well in this area.

7. Ask your child to show you the road test for chapter 7. Once again, congratulate and praise your child for the hard work he or she did in this chapter.

Chapter 8: Learning to Control My Body and Stay Out of Kids' Jail

1. Ask your child to name some reasons to stay out of kids' jail. These reasons are listed in assignment 8A.

2. Ask your child to explain what a court

and a judge are. If your child doesn't understand those words, review their meanings.

3. Ask your child the best way to stay out of kids' jail. (The answer is, "never do anything illegal or against the law").

4. Ask your child to review the basic rules about sexual touching that are found in this chapter. Here are the basic rules:

   a. Never touch anybody in any way without getting permission first.

   b. Never use force, threats, presents, or bribes to get someone to do sexual touching with you.

   c. Never touch someone's private parts if the person is more than two years younger than you are, even if the person says it's okay.

   d. Never talk to younger children about sexual behavior.

   e. Never do sexual touching with family members.

   f. Never touch your own private parts except when you are alone in a private place like your bedroom or the bathroom.

   g. Never do anything that hurts another person.

5. Have your child test you by reading assignment 8B together. Your child should already know the answers, since his or her counselor has already reviewed it. By doing this, your child will gain confidence in what he or she has learned.

6. *Roadmaps* teaches about the importance of always controlling our bodies in healthy ways. Ask your child what he or she wrote in assignment 8C, which asks for a description of some things the child has done in the past two weeks in which he or she did not control his or her body as well as should have happened.

7. Have your child review assignment 8E with you. The child already knows the answers, so this gives you a chance to reinforce the concepts that your child has learned.

8. Ask your child to show you the road test for chapter 8. As before, congratulate and praise your child for the hard work done in this chapter.

Chapter 9: Understanding the Four Wrong Turns to Wrong Touching

1. Ask your child to explain what a bad map is. *Roadmaps* teaches that a bad map is any bad learning experience that a child has when young.

2. Tell your child that this chapter is very hard to complete. Ask how your child feels about getting the chapter done. Give praise and support for the hard work it took to get though the chapter.

3. Ask your child what a body need is. *Roadmaps* teaches that body needs have to do with staying alive. They include things like being safe and warm and fed. Body needs include things like food, water, clothes, a good place to sleep, medicine when you need it, dental care, and someone to help you take care of yourself. While sex is an important and good part of life, it is not a real body need because a person can live without sex. You can't live without a true body need.

4. Ask your child what an emotional need is. *Roadmaps* teaches that emotional needs have to do with feeling loved, needed, and wanted. Research has shown that emotional needs are almost as important as body needs in staying alive and staying healthy. Emotional needs also have to do with believing in yourself and feeling like you are a capable and worthwhile person. Things like compliments, hugs, and smiles help

meet your emotional needs. So does getting good grades or being good at drawing or baseball or music or many other things that matter to you, *including* sex. Sex is not a true emotional need, but sex can be a very good thing for helping to balance a person's emotional needs when the person is an adult.

5. Ask your child what a roadblock is. *Roadmaps* teaches that roadblocks are things that affect you in the present. For example, Rita's parents didn't take care of her, and they sexually abused her. In that way they gave her a bad map when she was young, because they taught her that it was okay to do sexual things with children. Rita has found that she has several roadblocks that have resulted from her bad map. One roadblock is that she doesn't trust adults, and another is that she thinks about sexual touching all the time. These roadblocks are causing her lots of problems right now in her present life. Roadblocks make our lives difficult, and they slow down our healthy progress.

6. Ask your child what happened to Rita when she was a young child. Ask how those things affected Rita.

7. Ask your child to let you look at his or her answers to the assignment in which your child is asked to think about the different homes he or she has lived and then to figure out how his or her body needs and emotional needs were met and were not met in those homes. This is a good chance to validate your child's feelings and to provide emotional support and praise for the hard work of remembering painful past experiences.

8. Ask your child what a danger zone is. *Roadmaps* teaches that a danger zone is an unhealthy or unsafe living situation.

9. Ask your child to show you the road test for chapter 9. Chapter 9 was an extremely difficult chapter, so make sure that you congratulate and praise your child for the hard work it took to complete this chapter.

Chapter 10: Keeping Yourself and Others Safe with Good Rules and Good Boundaries

1. Ask your child what he or she learned about Josie's safety rules. Ask what some of the rules were.

2. Ask to see the list of special safety rules your child developed in assignment 10A. You may want to suggest additional rules, but make sure you give lots of praise for the rules your child did develop. You may want to help your child fill in assignment 10B, or suggest other people who could also review the rules.

3. Ask to see assignment 10C, and go ahead and sign and date the agreement. Help your child get other important people on his or her support team to also review and sign it.

4. Ask your child what a boundary is. *Roadmaps* teaches that boundaries are like fences people put around things they want to keep private (meaning keeping the thing just for themselves) or that they want treated a certain way. People can put boundaries around things or places, such as an iPod, clothes, a treatment notebook, or a bedroom. People can also have boundaries around their own bodies, with respect to how other people can touch them or how close others can be to them. People can also put boundaries around their own feelings or their past experiences. Sometimes people don't like to talk about their father, mother, or childhood because it makes them feel bad. Boundaries can be physical

(things or places), emotional (feelings or experiences), or social (rules or customs).

5. Ask your child to share assignment 10D with you. It describes your child's own list of personal boundaries.

6. Assignment 10F asks your child to find out what another person's boundaries are at home. Ask if your child wants to do that assignment with you. If your child agrees, explain what things in your home are private. You may also want to mention boundaries like taking off shoes in the house or shutting bathroom doors.

7. Assignment 10G is a daily boundary practice form. Your child might need some help filling out the form at the end of each day. You or your child's counselor should make copies of the blank form. By talking about boundaries and filling out this form, your child will become more aware of what boundaries are, and that will allow your child to become more sensitive to boundary issues in his or her everyday life. Your child may need to practice this skill and fill out the form for many weeks in order to properly teach and reinforce the concept.

8. Ask your child to show you the road test for chapter 10. This chapter was important, so make sure that you congratulate and praise your child for the hard work of completing this chapter. Also, make sure you continue to use the term "boundaries" in your daily life. Try to make positive comments whenever your child respects another person's boundaries. If your child violates another person's boundaries, give your child a gentle reminder.

Chapter 11: Talking about Touching That People Have Done to Me

1. What did Betty write about in her letter to her treatment group? (She wrote about being sexually abused by her stepdad.)

2. Ask if you can review assignment 11A. This assignment asks your child where he or she first learned about sexual touching. It can be very embarrassing or difficult for your child to talk about this topic, so make sure you give lots of praise.

3. Ask your child to look at assignment 11C, and ask who your child can talk to about personal feelings.

4. Ask if your child will show you assignment 11D, where your child drew a picture of someone touching him or her in a sexual way. This assignment can be a very personal or difficult one so give lots of praise and compliments as your child talks about this topic with you.

5. Ask your child to show you the road test for chapter 11. This chapter, just like many other chapters, was very important. Make sure that you congratulate and praise your child for the very hard work done in this chapter. From this day forward, try to reinforce your child's "survivor" behaviors.

Chapter 12: Telling the Truth About My Wrong Touching

1. Ask your child if you can review assignment 12A. It is a very personal assignment.

2. Ask your child why keeping secrets about wrong touching is not a good idea. *Roadmaps* teaches that keeping secrets about sexual touching is not good. It's like a garbage can that's overflowing with trash. Not only can it get stinky, but it takes a lot of energy to

keep the lid on those secrets. Keeping secrets about wrong touching doesn't help you stop. Keeping those secrets is like a false road sign that will probably send a child directly to kids' jail.

3. Ask your child to review his or her reasons for not telling the truth (assignment 12A) and his or her reasons for telling the truth (assignment 12B). Praise your child's reasons for telling the truth.

4. Ask your child if you can read assignment 12D. This is a very personal and embarrassing assignment, so give lots of encouragement. If you read it silently to yourself, you can save your child some shame and discomfort. If you think of anything your child left out, suggest that it be added. If your child doesn't want to share this assignment, respect that boundary and talk about the assignment with your child's counselor. The counselor can probably provide you with some ways you can help your child feel more comfortable about sharing this topic with you.

5. Ask your child to show you the road test for chapter 12. This chapter was very stressful and difficult, so again make sure that you congratulate and praise your child for the very hard work done in this chapter.

Chapter 13: Understanding How I Have Hurt People and Apologizing for My Wrong Touching

1. Tell your child that you understand that chapter 13 is all about apologizing to others for hurtful things that have been done to them. Ask your child about the letter that Kaitlyn wrote to her brother, Karl. Ask how your child felt about the letter, and what was good about the letter.

2. Ask your child to share the letter that he or she wrote for assignment 13B. Give your child some positive feedback about the letter. Talk with your child about whether or not it makes sense to send the letter to the person who was hurt, or to the person's parent or therapist. When the person who was hurt was a family member, the letters are often sent to the victim's therapist so that the victim may read them, but only when the therapist decides the time is right. When the person who was hurt was not a relative, it may not be advisable to send the letter, because the victim's parents may not want any contact with the person who abused their child. There may even be a restraining order against such contact. This issue should be discussed with your child's therapist; each decision about sending a letter is unique to that person's behavior and circumstances.

3. Congratulate your child on starting to make things better for the person who was hurt. Tell your child that you are proud he or she is becoming a member of the Sexual Abuse Prevention and Safety Team.

4. Ask your child to show you the road test for chapter 13. Apologizing for past wrong actions is sometimes very difficult, but it's a very big step in treatment. Make sure your child knows how very proud you are of his or her work on this chapter.

Chapter 14: Learning to Be a Survivor

1. Ask your child what a victim is. Also ask your child what a survivor is. In *Roadmaps*, victims are defined as people who don't get over the bad things that happen to them. For example, a person who is shot and killed during a robbery is a true victim. No matter what, that person is dead and

will not be coming back to life. In real life, most bad experiences do not result in death. That means it is possible to recover from bad experiences and move on through life to have many more good experiences. Survivors overcome their bad experiences and travel on to live good and healthy lives. Victims are called by that name when they cannot overcome their bad or traumatic experiences and end up acting out their trauma in negative ways. Ask your child to show you the chart in this chapter that illustrates the difference between victims and survivors.

2. Ask your child to test you on what you know about victims and survivors. Ask your child to show you assignment 14A. Have your child read the situations to you or help your child read them to you. Then try to answer the questions. Your child should already have received the correct answers from his or her counselor, so this discussion will give your child another chance to teach you about this concept and build self-confidence.

3. Ask your child if past abuse determines a person's future. In *Roadmaps*, children are taught that everyone has choices, and the choices really decide our future.

4. Ask your child to share assignment 14B with you. In that assignment your child listed his or her victim behaviors, as well as his or her survivor behaviors. The goal is to do fewer of the victim behaviors and do more of the survivor behaviors. Convince your child that you will do whatever you can to help him or her act like a survivor, if he or she has ever had a personal abuse experience or has experienced a significant life trauma.

5. Ask your child if he or she feels safe enough to share assignment 14C with you. This assignment is where your child describes a situation in which he or she felt hurt by someone. Make sure you thank your child for sharing, and try to empathize with the child's experience. In order words, tell your child that you understand how hard it must have been to go through that hurtful experience.

6. Ask your child to share the letter he or she wrote to a person who hurt him or her in assignment 14D. Thank your child for being willing to share such a personal letter.

7. Ask your child to show you the road test for chapter 14. Learning to be a survivor can be a lifelong challenge. Tell your child that you are going to do everything you can to help him or her become a true survivor.

Chapter 15: Recognizing My Early Warning Signs and Using My Umbrellas

1. Ask your child what an early warning sign is. In *Roadmaps*, an early warning sign is anything that a person feels or thinks or does that signals he or she is heading toward wrong or inappropriate sexual behavior. Early warning signs are different for each boy or girl. For example, thinking about a younger child's private parts might be a signal that the child doing the thinking would like to touch the other child's private parts. That would definitely be an early warning sign.

2. Ask your child to share assignment 15A, which is a list of his or her early warning signs.

3. Ask your child how an umbrella is defined in *Roadmaps*. *Roadmaps* teaches that learning to spot early warning signs is like knowing to check the skies for dark clouds and gray skies overhead

and always being prepared to bring out an umbrella when it starts to rain cats and dogs. In real life, umbrellas protect us from the rain. In *Roadmaps*, "umbrellas" are positive, healthy behaviors that protect us from life's rainstorms. Umbrellas are things we can use when we see dark clouds and gray skies overhead—our early warning signs. They help us get past bad times, bad thoughts, and bad feelings by making good choices. Umbrellas help to get us out of problem behaviors and send us in a positive, healthy direction.

4. Ask your child to share assignment 15B, which is a list of positive behaviors—umbrellas—that your child can use to interrupt negative behaviors or thoughts, like when early warning signs appear.

5. Ask your child to share assignment 15C with you, which is a personal list of your child's early warning signs and at least one umbrella for each of them. This list offers the beginning of a positive plan your child can implement to deal with negative thoughts in a healthy way. Tell your child that you fully support him or her and that you will help support the plan spelled out in 15C.

6. Ask your child to share assignment 15D, which is a list of other problem behaviors that your child would benefit from addressing. Review your child's efforts to find early warning signs and umbrellas for each of those behaviors listed in assignment 15E.

7. Ask your child to show you the road test for chapter 15. Learning how to identify early warning signs and umbrellas can be difficult. Remember these terms, and try to tell your child that you are going to help him or her practice these skills. Right now is a

good time to reinforce the idea that doing this work means your child will be a survivor rather than a victim.

Chapter 16: Making and Using My Safety Plan Book

1. Tell your child that you understand that chapter 16 has no road test. The "final exam" for *Roadmaps* is not a test; it is instead the making of a Safety Plan Book and practicing everything learned in *Roadmaps*. *Roadmaps* teaches that making it through the book is only the first part of your journey. The critical next step is for your child to keep using everything he or she has learned. If your child forgets the lessons learned in your child keeps practicing the lessons learned in *Roadmaps*, it truly will allow for a happy and healthy life.

2. By now, you have probably seen and reviewed your child's safety plan book. You may even have helped organize, decorate, and add new pages to the plan. Regardless of whether you have seen the plan or not, now is a great time to ask your child to show it to you, so that you can review all of your child's work, even if you saw the plan in an earlier stage. Discuss with your child who else should be shown the book. The idea is that the more people in a child's support team, the more support the child will receive for making good, healthy choices.

3. The most important part of this chapter is keeping the Safety Plan Book alive and useful. This basically means periodically opening up the book, adding new pages, and talking about the skills and rules that have been established there. Congratulate your child on putting together a beautiful and helpful plan.

Roadmaps is finished, but support, supervision, and practice of skills will continue for many years. Without practice, skills will erode over time, so it is a parent's job to keep solid boundaries in the home, maintain solid supervision, and give ongoing praise for your child's efforts to learn and maintain a healthy lifestyle.

This would be a good time to take your child out to dinner or plan some other fun activity to reward his or her work.

Remind your child once again that finishing *Roadmaps* doesn't mean treatment is over. Tell your child it's now time to show that he or she has made progress in treatment by remembering the lessons and information learned in *Roadmaps* and maintaining all the positive skills developed.

Questions to Ask Your Child As Treatment Progresses If Your Child Is Using the *Pathways* Workbook

It is important to remind your child that you also have a part to play in the treatment process. Explain that your job is to learn about some of the same things your child is learning. Set aside time each week to ask what your child is working on in *Pathways*. Ask your child to tell you whenever he or she has completed a chapter, so that you can spend a little time learning about treatment. As each chapter is completed, set aside some private time to review the following questions with your child. You can ask your child's counselor to do this with you for the first several chapters in order to increase your comfort level and your child's comfort level.

Chapter 1: Discuss Court, Evaluation, and Initial Reactions
Among other questions, you can ask your child such questions as:
1. "Why does it help to admit to all of your sexual behavior during the evaluation and court process?"
2. "How far do you have to go, or what do you have to do to another person, before a sexual act can be called rape?"
3. "Why is what you did wrong?"
4. "What is true consent?"
5. "What are the building blocks of a consensual relationship?"
6. "Have you received a list of sexual assault laws for this state or country?" If the answer is yes, ask to see a copy and become familiar with them.
7. "Can you test me by reading the legal or illegal situations in chapter 1?" Have your child tell you if you are correct or incorrect. This is a good way to reinforce your child's awareness of the sexual assault laws.
8. "Can you share with me what types of pornography you have seen in your life?" By starting to talk about this issue, you build rapport and show your support for the treatment process.

Chapter 2: Discuss Treatment Goals and How He or She Can Become a Group Member
Ask your child such questions as:
1. "What is your personal list of problems and goals?" Remember, at least one of the goals and problems on the list should relate to the child's sexual behavior problems.
2. "How does your treatment group work?"
3. "What are the rules in your group?"
4. "What regular assignments do you have in your group?"
5. "How can I help you with your requirement to write every day in a diary or journal? Is there a time in the evening that I can help you set aside to do your treatment work?"
6. "Can you help me understand what an anger iceberg is?"

This is a good time to establish some regular communication about issues that are discussed in the treatment group. Some programs ask that names of other group members be kept confidential, even though most programs want clients to talk with their parents about general issues and what they are learning in the group. It is a good idea to talk with your child's counselor about how to handle this issue. Many teenagers tell their parents that they can't talk about what happens in the group, but in many cases the youth is simply practicing avoidance, and such a rule may not even exist.

Chapter 3: Discuss Disclosing

Questions you can ask your child include:

1. "What were your reasons for denying parts of your behavior at first?"
2. "On a scale of 0–100 percent, how much of your problem behavior have you now disclosed?"
3. "What were your reasons for deciding to tell the truth about your behavior?"
4. "What is a thinking error?" Review the list of thinking errors from chapter 3.
5. "Can you explain what a distant elephant is?"
6. "Have you completed your sexual history with your group?"
7. "I understand there are three stages of denial for people with sexual problems. Can you explain them to me? Which stage are you in?"
8. "Are there behaviors in your sexual history that I don't know about yet that you will need to share with me later?" If the child answers yes, then ask, "When do you think you will be ready to do that?"

Chapter 4: Discuss Learning About Victims

Ask the following questions and any others that feel relevant:

1. "What are some myths about sexual abuse?"
2. "What happened to Donnie? How did you feel listening to that story?"

3. "What is a physical boundary? What are your physical boundaries?"
4. "What is an emotional boundary? What are your emotional boundaries?"
5. "What is a social boundary?"
6. "What have you learned about how victims feel?"
7. "Have you started your Healthy Living Project yet?"
8. "What kind of sexual harassment have you observed at your school?"

Chapter 5: Discuss "Why I Did It"

For your child to understand his or her sexual acting-out, ask the following:

1. "Where do you think your motivation to act out sexually came from?"
2. "Can you tell me about your internal barriers and how you overcame them?"
3. "What external barriers would have helped you not act out sexually?"
4. "How did you overcome the victim's resistance?"
5. "What is self-talk?"

Chapter 6: Discuss How to Identify Grooming and Maintenance Behaviors

One discussion opener could include, "There are a lot of new terms to learn here. It would help me to understand your treatment if we could talk about those terms." Ask your child:

1. "What is a grooming behavior?"
2. "What is a maintenance behavior?"
3. "What is a gateway behavior?"
4. "What are your maintenance behaviors?"
5. "What grooming behaviors did you use when you were acting out?"

Chapter 7: Discuss Understanding the Chain of Events that Led to Your Child's Sexual Behavior Problems

Ask the following and any other relevant questions:

1. "What events were happening in

your life before you started to act out sexually?"

2. "What behaviors were you engaging in before you started to act out sexually? If we can look at those, maybe we can fix the problem before you start to act out again." This is a good time to add your thoughts about your child's list of behaviors that may have led up to the child's sexual misconduct.

3. "What feelings do you think you were having before you started to act out?"

4. "What are thinking-error bridges? Can you tell me about yours yet?"

5. "Can you explain your offense behavior chain?"

6. "Can I help you figure out your timeline for your behavior problems?"

Chapter 8: Discuss Controlling and Expressing Sexual Feelings in Positive Ways

Ask the following or other questions of your child:

1. "With everyone trying so hard to help you, it might be difficult to admit if you're still having urges to act out sexually. It won't hurt anyone's feelings if you are still having urges. In fact, you might have these urges every once in a while for a long time. But if you let us know when it's happening, we can help. Are you having such urges? When was the last time you had such an urge?"

2. "Do you talk with your counselor about your sexual urges and feelings?"

3. "Can you help me understand the difference between impulse control and arousal control?"

4. "What is thought stopping?"

5. "What is CS?"

6. "Are you using CS in your treatment?"

An optional comment you can say to your child: "I know that you have a form to fill out to keep track of when you masturbate. I won't ask you about it, but I want you to know that it is okay with me that you masturbate, as long as you are honest about it with your counselor."

Chapter 9: Discuss Creating and Following a Relapse Prevention Plan

1. "I'd like you to explain to me what your personal warning signs are."

2. "What is your prevention plan for each of your warning signs?"

3. "What is a lapse?"

4. "What is a relapse?"

5. "What is a high-risk situation, a HRS (pronounced 'hearse')?"

6. "What is a SUD (seemingly unimportant decision)?"

7. "Who has signed your prevention plan so far?"

Chapter 10: Discuss Understanding Sexual Abuse and Other Traumatic Life Experiences

1. "I'm sure there are a lot of things you've gone through that I don't know about, but I'd like to know. Can you talk to me about the ways you feel you have been verbally, emotionally, physically, or sexually abused?"

2. "How have those experiences affected you? What are some ways you numbed out? Tried to fight? Tried to escape or get out of that situation or those feelings (flight)?"

3. "How do you think being abused contributed to your acting out?"

4. "May I look at what you have done in your Healthy Living Project so far?"

Chapter 11: Discuss Clarification: Making Things Clear and Apologizing for My Behavior

1. "What is this clarification process about?"

2. "Would you let me read your clarification letters to the parents and the victim?"

3. "Can you help me understand what was wrong with Brandon's clarification letter?"

4. "Are you thinking about sending a letter or meeting with the victim or the victim's parents? Have you talked with your counselor about it? If there is a meeting, would you like me to come with you?"

Chapter 12: Discuss Steps to Personal Accountability: Becoming an Honest, Responsible, Sensitive Person Who Has Integrity

1. "Who have your decided to talk with about your sexual problem?" (Step 1)

2. "Who in your life do you think can support your treatment efforts? When will you talk to that person about your treatment?" (Step 2)

3. "Do you want my feedback about your day-to-day behavior?" (Step 3)

4. "Who are you writing your honesty letters to?" (Step 4) Give positive feedback for good choices.

5. "What costs and benefits of your sexual acting-out did you come up with?" (Step 5)

6. "What are some ways you've been taking responsibility for your actions lately?" (Step 6) Optional comment: "I've noticed some things, but maybe I don't see all of them."

7. "How do you think your sexual behavior affected other people?" (Step 7)

8. "What is empathy? How can you show empathy for the victim?" (Step 8)

9. "Would you share your list of people you plan to make amends to? What will you do to make amends? Do you need any help figuring out ways to make amends?" (Step 9) Optional comment: "I respect you for trying to make things better. It's a real sign of integrity."

10. "How do you think we could make our relationship healthier?" (Step 10)

11. "Would you like my feedback about your honest, responsible, and nonvictimizing behavior?" (Step 11)

12. "Who are you talking to about the steps to accountability? If you write a draft letter to a newspaper editor, I'd like to read it." (Step 12)

13. "Are you willing to share your victim perspective assignment from Step 8 with me?" Hearing this assignment can be very difficult. Clients often share very detailed information about how the abuse occurred that you were not aware of. Be prepared for the emotional reaction you may have. This assignment might best be shared in the counselor's office.

Chapter 13: Completing Their STOP Plan
Ask the following question:

1. "I know you need to review your STOP Plan with me. Would you like to share it now?" Feel free to give your child suggestions about things to add to the STOP Plan, if they come to mind while you are reviewing it. This is a good time to praise your adolescent for his or her hard work in *Pathways*!

Chapter 14: Discuss Completing Treatment by Living a Responsible and Healthy Lifestyle
Ask the following questions:

1. "Can you tell me what Phillip's problem was? Are there things you're doing where you use the same kinds of thinking and feel the same ways as when you acted out sexually?"

2. "What does 'denial of the continuing problem' mean?"

3. "Would you be willing to share your self-letter with me?"

4. "Now that you have completed *Pathways*, are you cured? How can we

work together to help you never reoffend now that this part of your treatment is done?"

5. "May I read your chapter 14 final examination report?"

Chapter 14: Discuss Your Child's Healthy Living Project

Ask the following question:

1. "Will you please show me your Healthy Living Project?" As you review the project, feel free to give suggestions about how to improve it. As you look through the Healthy Living Project notebook it is often helpful to give suggestions about how to make the notebook more attractive or organized. Sometimes parents can provide pictures of their child engaged in a healthy activity that can then be included in the Healthy Living Project. Make sure you say some positive things about your child's work on this assignment. The Healthy Living Project is a type of culminating project that takes a great deal of time and effort to complete.

Recommended Readings

Most of the books on this list are available at local bookstores or on the Internet. Some are available from the Safer Society Press (www.safersociety.org). A few others are available only by writing to the publisher at the address given.

Bell, Ruth. *Changing Bodies, Changing Lives.* New York: Three Rivers Press, 1998. Available from Safer Society Press.

Bonner, Barbara. *Taking Action: Support for Families of Adolescents with Illegal Sexual Behavior.* Brandon, VT: Safer Society Press, 2010.

Brohl, K., and J. C. Potter. When Your Child Has Been Molested: A Parent's Guide to Healing and Recovery. Rev. ed. San Francisco: Jossey-Bass, 2004.

Cavanaugh Johnson, T. *Helping Children with Sexual Behavior Problems: A Guidebook for Professionals and Caregivers.* San Diego: Institute on Violence Abuse and Trauma, 2009. Available from Safer Society Press.

Cavanagh Johnson, T. *Understanding Children's Sexual Behaviors: What's Natural and Healthy.* San Diego: Institute on Violence Abuse and Trauma, 2010. Available from Safer Society Press.

MacFarlane, Kee, and Carolyn Cunningham. *Steps to Healthy Touching.* Indianapolis: Kidsrights, 2003.

Madaras, L. *Ready, Set, Grow? A "What's Happening to My Body?" Book for Younger Girls.* New York: Newmarket Press, 2003.

Madaras, L., and A. Madaras. *The What's Happening to My Body? Book for Boys. A Growing Up Guide for Parents and Sons.* New York: Newmarket Press, 2000.

Rich, Phil. *Understanding, Assessing and Rehabilitating Juvenile Sex Offenders.* Hoboken, N.J.: John Wiley and Sons, 2003.

Ryan, Gail, Tom Leversee, and Sandy Lane. *Juvenile Sexual Offending: Causes, Consequences, and Correction.* San Francisco: Jossey-Bass, 2010.

Shoop, Robert J. *Sexual Exploitation in Schools: How to Spot It and Stop It.* Thousand Oaks, CA: Corwin Press, 2004.

Silovsky, Jane. *Taking Action: Support for Families of Children with Sexual Behavior Problems.* Brandon, VT: Safer Society Press, 2009.

Steen, Charlene. *Choices, A Relapse Prevention Workbook for Female Offenders.* Brandon, VT: Safer Society Press, 2006.

Van Dam, Carla. *Identifying Child Molesters: Preventing Child Sexual Abuse by Recognizing the Patterns of the Offenders.* New York: The Haworth Press, 2001.

Wiehe, Vernon. *The Brother/Sister Hurt: Recognizing the Effects of Sibling Abuse.* Brandon, VT: Safer Society Press, 1996.

Wurtele, Sandy, and Feather Berkower. *Off Limits: Keeping Kids and Teens Safe from Sexual Abuse.* Brandon, VT: Safer Society Press, 2010.

About the Author

Timothy J. Kahn is a nationally recognized clinician and trainer in the field of sexual offender treatment. In Washington State, he is a licensed Clinical Independent Social Worker, a Licensed Mental Health Counselor, and a Certified Sexual Offender Treatment Provider.

His book, *Pathways: A Guided Workbook for Youth Beginning Treatment*, now in its fourth edition, has served as a valuable treatment tool in both outpatient and residential programs across the United States and in other parts of the world. His other guided workbook, *Roadmaps*, second edition, provides a framework for the treatment of young people with sexual behavior problems.

Mr. Kahn is a Clinical Assistant Professor with the University of Washington School of Social Work. He served as the chairman of the Washington State Sex Offender Treatment Provider Advisory Committee, which has developed evaluation and treatment standards and licensing requirements for counselors treating adolescent and adult sex offenders in Washington. He has been instrumental in the development of training and treatment programs in British Columbia and Washington State, and he regularly consults with a number of residential treatment agencies and foster care agencies in the Pacific Northwest. Most importantly, he is the father of three boys and the grandfather of two young girls and one young boy.

Mr. Kahn currently maintains a private clinical and consultation practice in Bellevue, Washington, where he evaluates and treats children, adolescents, and adults with sexual behavior problems.

Safer Society Foundation and Safer Society Press

The Safer Society Foundation, Inc. is a private, non-profit agency working to end sexual abuse and its detrimental effects on society. We believe sexual abuse is a public health issue whose solution can only be found in an integrated, system-wide approach. To this end, we seek collaborative partnerships with treatment providers, the legal system, mental health agencies, survivors, educators, parents — everyone with a stake in this crucial issue.

Safer Society Press is the publishing program of the Safer Society Foundation. Please visit the web site to learn more about other Safer Society Press titles.

P.O. Box 340, Brandon, Vermont 05733
802-247-3132
www.safersociety.org